W9-CUF-978

Attention Deficit Disorder: Hyperactivity Revisited

A Concise Source of Information for Parents and Teachers

H. Moghadam

Detselig Enterprises Ltd.
Calgary, Alberta

© 1988 **H. Moghadam,** M.D., M.P.H., F.R.C.P.C.
  Professor of Pediatrics and Community Medicine
  University of Calgary
  Consulting Pediatrician, Alberta Children's Hospital
  Calgary, Alberta

with contributions by:

S. Gupta, Ed.D.
  Psychologist, Alberta Children's Hospital
  Calgary, Alberta

M. Haug, Ph.D.
  Clinical Psychologist, Alberta Children's Hospital
  Calgary, Alberta

C. McFee, M.S.W., Social Worker
  Alberta Children's Hospital
  Calgary, Alberta

Canadian Cataloguing in Publication Data

Moghadam, H. (Hossein)
  Attention deficit disorder : hyperactivity
revisited

  ISBN 0-920490-78-6

  1. Attention deficit disorders. 2.
Hyperactive children. I. Title.
RJ496.A86M64 1988   618.92′8589   C88-091206-5

Detselig Enterprises Ltd.
P.O. Box G 399
Calgary, Alberta, Canada T3A 2G3

All rights reserved. No part of this book may be reproduced in
any form or by any means without permission in writing from
the publisher.

Printed in Canada   SAN 115-0324   ISBN 0-920490-78-6

This book is dedicated to the parents and teachers of hyperactive and other misunderstood children

A Disclaimer

This book is a very concise source of information on attention deficit disorder and as such does not attempt to completely cover this complex and controversial topic. Although every attempt has been made to present all sides of the controversy, the brevity of presentation has precluded attention to the details. This book is not intended to be a substitute for your physician's advice. Every child with attention deficit disorder is an unique individual and his/her management must be tailored to suit the child's needs, as well as the needs of the family and teacher. Neither the author nor the publisher accept any legal or moral responsibility, nor any liability, for actions taken by parents which may be contrary to the advice of their physician.

Brand names of medications have been included in the book because, normally, parents and teachers are not familiar with the drugs' generic names. This is not to be construed, however, as an endorsement or a criticism of these or other products. Statements regarding the therapeutic properties, the effectiveness, and the side effects of drugs are based entirely on the author's experience and may differ from the experience of other physicians.

Acknowledgments

The author and contributors wish to thank Ms. Rosanne Fortini-Burrows for her patience and tolerance while the preparation of this book was undertaken.

Dr. Moghadam wishes to also thank Dr. Bonnie Kaplan, Director, Behavioral Research Unit, Alberta Children's Hospital. Her reviewing of several chapters of this book, practical comments and suggestions were a tremendous help and are sincerely appreciated.

Pictures drawn by Heather Sawyer

Detselig Enterprises Ltd. appreciates the financial assistance for its 1988 publishing program from

Alberta Foundation for the Literary Arts
Canada Council
Department of Communications
Alberta Culture

Contents

Preface

The behavior disorder which is known as hyperactivity has been with us since time immemorial. It is a relatively common problem affecting on the average, one child in every classroom in North America. Excessive activity is seen in "normal" children as well as children with a variety of psychological disorders; however, the term hyperactivity has been used to designate a specific childhood disorder consisting of chronic inattention, impulsivity, purposeless overactivity, difficulties with social interaction, and a number of associated symptoms. Over the past several decades many different names have been given to this entity. Since 1980, the scientific community has preferred to use *attention deficit disorder*. It is now believed that the core symptom is an inherent weakness in the ability to concentrate on relevant tasks and to maintain attention until the task is completed. There are, however, still some investigators who believe that even this designation does not adequately describe the disorder, notwithstanding the fact that attentional difficulties are always present in hyperactive children.

Perhaps the most unnecessarily alarming name was an old one which considered the affected children to be brain damaged. Fortunately, that label, *minimal brain damage,* was eventually replaced by a less unpleasant one, *minimal brain dysfunction.* Although it is true that some children with a clear-cut history of brain insult or damage manifest similar behaviors as hyperactive children, the vast majority of children suffering from attention deficit disorder have no history of such insult or damage.

Throughout this book we use hyperactivity or hyperactive behavior disorder (HA), attention deficit disorder (ADD) and attention-deficit hyperactivity disorder (ADHD) interchangeably since all terms are currently in use and refer to the same

1

entity. It is quite likely that as we gain more knowledge about the disorder, we may yet give it a different name in the future.

Although attention deficit disorder is seen in individuals of all ages, we will confine our discussion to the disorder in children.

The impetus for writing this book was provided by the parents and teachers of hyperactive children attending our clinic, and their request for a concise source of information on attention deficit disorder, and the rationale for the recommended approaches to its treatment. As such this book is not intended to be a scientific discourse or the final word on hyperactivity. Rather, it is a short presentation of what is currently known, and it should provide the readers with sufficient information and the various perspectives to enable them to make informed decisions.

Although controversial issues are discussed in the book, we do not provide specific references to scientific journals with respect to these issues. Instead, we provide the interested reader with a short list of additional readings which review these issues in more detail and may be readily available in the local public or college libraries. Despite our attempt to refrain from using scientific jargon, occasionally we have found it necessary and therefore have bracketed it within the text.

A Brief Historical Review

Our youth now loves luxury. They have bad manners, contempt for authority and disrespect for their elders. Children nowadays are tyrants.

Socrates
470 –399 B.C.

The earliest known description of hyperactive behavior in a child was published in the 1845 children's storybook *"Der Struwwelpeter (Unkempt Peter),"* by German physician Dr. Heinrich Hoffman. The particular story of interest within this volume is *Die Geschichte vom Zappel Philipp.* Some readers may be familiar with the entire translation which has been retained in its original doggerel verse. The first few lines are as follows:

> Fidgity Phil,
> He won't sit still,
> He wiggles,
> And giggles,
> At the dinner table,
> And when his father admonishes him,
> The naughty restless child,
> Grows still more rude and wild.

Toward the end of World War I many countries experienced an epidemic of brain infection (encephalitis), often associated with severe lethargy (sleeping sickness or Von Economo's encephalitis lethargica). Many of the adults who survived the acute illness later developed a disorder known as Parkinson's syndrome which consist of muscle rigidity, an abnormal gait, shaky arms and hands, expressionless face, drooling and disturbances of attention, memory, and emotion. On the other hand, some of the children who survived the acute illness developed a constellation of behavioral traits similar to what is now known as hyperactivity or attention-deficit hyperactivity disorder. This is the origin of the now discredited label *minimal brain damage.* However, it was soon realized that there were also many hyperactive children who did not suffer from encephalitis or otherwise show evidence of frank brain damage. Over the years, the label was replaced by *minimal brain dysfunction,* which still lingers in both the scientific literature and popular magazines.

In 1937 Dr. Charles A. Bradley, an American psychiatrist, described a group of institutionalized emotionally-disturbed children who responded to treatment with benzedrine, a stimulant drug. They showed increased interest in school work, better work habits, and an improvement in their disruptive behavior. This seemingly contradictory response of hyperactive children to stimulant drugs remained a debating point among researchers for some time. As will be seen later in this book, it is not contradictory at all.

During the 1960s and early 1970s there was a wave of overprescription of stimulant drugs for the treatment of all sorts of aberrant behaviors and school failures. This overprescription which, to a lesser extent, has persisted up to the present time, led to a justifiable outcry by many teachers, other professionals, parents, and even some physicians against "medicating" children for their behavior problems. However, the same protestation became an impetus for the vastly intensified research into the causes of ADHD and its treatment. We are still not quite certain why stimulant drugs improve the behavior of only some children with attention deficit disorder and not others. Hundreds of scientists around the world are searching for answers to this and many other questions on this complex problem.

2

Attention Deficit Disorder – What is it?

On every scientist's desk there is a drawer labeled "unknown" in which he files what are at the moment unsolved questions, lest through guesswork or impatient speculation he come upon incorrect answers that will do him more harm than good. Man's worst fault is opening the drawer too soon. His task is not to discover final answers but to win the best partial answers that he can, from which others may move confidently against the unknown, to win better ones.

Homer W. Smith
(1895 – 1962)

It is ironic that an abundance of writings on any topic, whether in scientific journals or in popular magazines, is often an indication of our inadequate understanding of that topic. Consider a well-known condition like poliomyelitis. Most young readers of this book have not seen a child afflicted by poliomyelitis, but know that it is a disease which can be prevented through routine immunization of children. Neither in scientific journals nor in popular magazines does one find articles about poliomyelitis. Now consider coronary heart disease or cancer which are two common killers. It is hardly possible to find a scientific journal or a popular magazine without an article on these diseases. When we learned all about poliomyelitis and its cause, we soon learned how to prevent it. It is no longer a major threat to our health and, therefore, it would be a waste of journal pages to write about it. Not so with heart disease and cancer. We still have a great deal to learn about them. As long as the search for their cause and prevention goes on, scientists publish the results of their investigations in professional journals. Attention deficit disorder belongs to the same league. Between 1957 and 1960, less than three dozen articles appeared in the scientific journals on the topic of hyperactivity. Twenty years later, between 1977 and 1980, over seven thousand articles were published on this same subject! The pace of research and publications during the past decade has not diminished. It is the most researched childhood behavioral disorder and yet much remains to be learned about it.

Seldom has a condition caused so much confusion and controversy among psychiatrists, neurologists, pediatricians, psychologists, educators, and the general public. Some reputable scientists even deny its very existence! Confusion and controversy have also reached the political arena, where attempts have been made to ban one or another form of treatment. Yet we have made remarkably slow progress in our understanding of its very nature. With each new piece of published research, it seems more questions are generated than are answered.

Does hyperactivity really exist? To the distraught parent,

or the harassed teacher, this is only an academic question. They know that it does. They experience it every day.

The hyperactive child, more often a boy than a girl, seems to be in constant motion, purposeless motion. He disrupts the classroom activities and distracts other children. He talks loudly, excessively, and out of turn. He interrupts others' conversation. When he does not talk, he often makes annoying noises. He seems to know the rules of appropriate behavior for his age, but somehow is not capable of following these rules. Even when he is repeatedly admonished for inappropriate behavior, he seems to repeat similar behavior over and over again. It is not that he is not motivated to comply with rules and social norms; he just seems to have a difficult time regulating his activities, emotions and thoughts. He often seems to daydream and not to listen even when he is talked to directly. Although ostensibly looking at his mother or teacher during conversations, at times he seems to be looking right through them, preoccupied with distant thoughts.

He often changes his activities, and seldom, if ever, completes any tasks. His work is sloppy, careless and pocked with excessive errors. In family games he is a poor loser and attempts to change the game rules in order to win. The same tendency to change the rules leads to his being left out of group games whether in school or in the neighborhood. This type of behavior makes it difficult for him to find and/or keep friends even though he craves friendship. With adults, he is often sassy. He is impulsive in style and acts without thinking. He will trip over objects, and bump into doors and walls more often than his expected share. When given a new toy, his first impulse is to take it apart. When trying to re–assemble it, he loses his patience and goes on to other activities.

He may have difficulty falling asleep and occasionally his sleep is restless. If a preschooler, he may wake up frequently during the night to explore the household. He is an early riser and frequently is not in a good mood upon arousal. Oddly enough, in one-to-one situations, such as in a physician's office, he seems to behave perfectly normally. Occasionally, however, he attempts to make the physician's office look like a battle zone. He is often moody and has a low frustration tolerance. As a result, he may show temper outbursts, with tendencies to bully and fight other children. His school performance is often poor and he has low self-esteem.

The foregoing is a portrait of a typical hyperactive child. Hyperactive children, however, are a diverse group of individuals who seldom exhibit the complete array of abnormal behavior described above. Even in the same hyperactive child, the intensity of abnormal behavior varies from time to time and from situation to situation. In fact, the usual pattern is an inconsistency of the behavior.

Most of the behavior problems common to these children emanate from inattention, impulsivity, and hyperactivity at a level which is inappropriate for their age. Obviously one cannot expect a two-year-old child to be as attentive to a learning task as a seven- year-old child. Nor does one expect him to be reflective in his behavior or sit quietly in a corner for long. However, a significant number of "hyperactive" children, although displaying much of the above mentioned behaviors, are not physically hyperactive. For this reason, many professionals use *attention deficit disorder;* believing that the core problem of the affected children is impaired attention rather than hyperactivity.

Impaired attention makes it difficult for these children to focus and sustain their attention on a task and to resist distraction. Impulsivity makes it difficult for them to resist immediate temptations and modulate their behavior appropriately. Hyperactivity, when present, makes it difficult for them to regulate their activities, so that they will be purposeful and goal-oriented.

Although some or all of the above described behaviors are frequently seen in hyperactive children, some professionals question whether we are sufficiently precise in our definition of terms to be justified in calling the condition a distinct disorder by any name. They argue that both terms have resisted precise definition and cite some studies which have shown a relatively low level of agreement among parents, teachers and clinicians as to which children are hyperactive. While instruments for measurement of movements are available, there are no instruments which would precisely measure purposeless movements. When two different rating scales, usually questionnaires are used to identify hyperactive children, parents and teachers do not always pick out the same children, even if both questionnaires have been validated and tested for reliability on the normal childhood population. Similarly, children who seem to be inattentive and easily distracted in the classroom can be seen totally absorbed in their favorite television shows. Is it then an *attention* deficit which is troublesome to these children or rather an *application* deficit? The phrase, "If Johnny could only apply himself" is familiar to many teachers and parents alike. Some clinicians argue that a seemingly inattentive child is capable of tuning in but is, in fact, not motivated to do what is expected of him in accordance with the norms set for him by adults. He *chooses* not to apply himself.

Another source of disagreement among professional groups dealing with hyperactive children has been the difficulty distinguishing between attention deficit disorder and *conduct disorders* of childhood. Some clinicians believe that these are identical disorders. Others argue that the two groups of disorders have many overlapping features, but that conduct disorders are characterized by the predominance of callous antisocial behaviors with violation of the basic rights and property of others.

Some clinicians believe that there is little justification for coining a new name, that is, attention deficit disorder for what is not a distinct entity, since inattentiveness and restlessness are also seen commonly in association with a number of other conditions, notably learning disabilities. In response, other clinicians argue that there is a distinct difference between restlessness and inattention of children with attention deficit disorder (ADD) and those of learning-disabled children: The learning disabled children, unlike ADD children, are not inattentive and restless outside the classroom, and they were not so in their preschool years. Their restlessness and inattentiveness becomes apparent only when they are faced with academic activities.

The major difficulty with learning-disabled children is their apparent inability to adequately process auditory and/or visual information presented to them while they are being taught to read, write and do arithmetic. Because of this information- processing difficulty, the learning-disabled children become restless and inattentive only in the classroom, or at home when they are expected to do school-related homework. Their behavior in these situations can be compared with that of any of us who happens to be inadvertently present in a scientific meeting of scholars, discussing topics beyond the limit of our understanding. In these situations we too, may become restless and fidgity, with our minds wandering off to easier-to-handle thoughts. This daydreaming and restlessness, however, would not persist when we leave the scientific meeting.

What distinguishes the inattentiveness of hyperactive children from that of learning-disabled children is the omnipresence of their behavior. ADD children, in contrast to learning-disabled children, display abnormal behavior, with varying degrees of intensity, in all situations, that is, classroom, home, playground, supermarket, church and often in the physician's office. Furthermore, they have displayed this behavior even in their preschool years. It must be re- emphasized, that in spite of this pervasiveness across time and situation, the inconsistency of abnormal behavior, both in terms of their presence, or absence, and their intensity, is a hallmark of the disorder.

The inattentiveness of attention-deficit hyperactive disorder (ADHD) children is an intrinsic deficiency of their ability to focus their attention. It is a primary deficiency and is the cause of their learning problems. On the other hand, the inattentiveness of learning-disabled children is secondary to, and a result of, their information processing difficulties; unable to cope with printed words, their minds wander off the learning tasks and they become daydreamers.

Inattention can also be secondary to other factors such as depression and anxiety in the child, emotional disturbances in other family members, chaotic home environment, inappropriate expectation of the child by his parents or teachers, and occasionally, a conscious effort on the part of the child not to pay attention in order to avoid humiliation (application deficit). There are, of course, children with mixed types of inattention. This classification of chronic inattention into primary and secondary types has therapeutic implications in that only primary inattention and mixed primary and secondary types of inattention respond to medical treatment. Secondary types of inattention require different types of intervention. The following table may serve to further clarify this useful distinction between various types of chronic inattention.

Finally, it must be said that up to the present time, research has not made it clear whether attention deficit disorder is a single condition or a set of conditions. What is abundantly clear, however, is that hyperactive children are not a homogeneous group of individuals.

A General Classification of Chronic Inattention in School-Age Children

Subtypes	Description	Some Common Associations	Common Denominators
Primary attention deficit	Intrinsic inefficiencies of selective attention	Early onset of temperamental dysfunction Perinatal stress events Signs of neuromaturational delay Inattention in multiple settings and situations Sleep disorders	Purposeless selection Weak resistance to distraction.
Secondary attention deficit	Inattention secondary to deficits in information processing	Visual perceptual motor problems Developmental language disabilities Deficits of sequential organization and short-term memory Signs of neuromaturational delay	Impersistence. Inefficiencies of motor activity.
	Inattention secondary to psychosocial social and emotional disturbances	Family problems Emotional disturbance in other family members Primary depression and anxiety	Impulsivity. Academic Failure.
	Apparent inattention resulting from inappropriate expectations, perceptions, or educational circumstances extrinsic to the child	Tendency toward inattention only in specific settings or situations Strong foci of interest and competence Discrepant perceptions of child by adults	Social Failure. Performance inconsistency.
	Inattention as a conscious strategy	Task-specific attention weakness-"designed" to avoid humiliation	Diminished self-esteem.
Mixed	Two or more subtypes	Relevant to subtypes	Insatiability.

Modified from Levine, Melvin D. et al.

3

How Prevalent is Attention Deficit Disorder?

It should be clear from the foregoing discussion that it is difficult to talk about the prevalence of attention deficit disorder when there is poor agreement among scientists on what the disorder is. The American Psychiatric Association has attempted to devise diagnostic criteria for attention deficit disorder with or without hyperactivity and differentiate it from other disruptive behaviors of childhood. The first such attempt was made in 1981 in the third edition of the

Diagnostic and Statistical Manual, "DSM III." This manual recognized three major types of attention deficit disorder: ADD with hyperactivity; consisting of inattention, impulsivity and hyperactivity; ADD without hyperactivity; and ADD residual type, which described young adults (18 years of age and older) who have a history of childhood ADD, with or without hyperactivity, and whose signs and symptoms have persisted in varying degrees into adulthood. In 1987 a revised edition of this manual was published and included a revision of the diagnostic criteria for this disorder (see Chapter 5) which is now known as attention-deficit hyperactivity disorder (ADHD).

The published studies of the prevalence of attention deficit disorder have not always used the above diagnostic criteria. Nor is it always clear that, when used, how strictly the criteria were adhered to in order to arrive at the diagnosis. It is then not surprising that different prevalence rates have been found by different investigators. Furthermore, since hyperactivity, inattention and impulsivity tend to change with maturity, different prevalence rates are obtained if some investigators study only kindergarten to Grade 4 students, and others include children in junior high school as well.

Another confounding difficulty in establishing prevalence rates is related to the fact that many more boys suffer from this disorder than girls. If all children are pooled together a different prevalence rate is obtained than when only boys are studied. For example, a study conducted in Italy reported 20% of boys and 3% of girls were hyperactive. However, the combined rate for all children when boys and girls were pooled was 12%.

Many prevalence studies use standardized questionnaires for parents and teachers to rate hyperactive behaviors. Some questionnaires require the parent or teacher to respond whether a particular symptom, say inattention, is present sometimes, often, or always. Other questionnaires require the parent or teacher to respond whether the child displays a particular symptom not at all, a little, pretty much, or very much.

It can be seen that using various techniques to establish the prevalence of this disorder will produce different results. Nonetheless, when similar techniques are used, there seems to be general agreement in different studies reported from various countries. About 2 – 3% of girls and 6 – 9% of boys are reported to be hyperactive in studies conducted in the United States, Great Britain, Australia, Germany and China. Somewhat higher prevalence rates are reported from Italy, Spain and New Zealand.

It is apparent that attention deficit disorder, whether or not accompanied by hyperactivity, is a common childhood behavior disorder. The question is how to diagnose and differentiate it from similar behavior disorders which require different approaches to their treatment. This will be discussed in Chapter 5. Before getting into the discussion of the diagnosis, however, we will briefly discuss the suspected causes of attention-deficit hyperactivity disorder.

4

What Causes
Attention Deficit Disorder?

There are in fact two things, science and opinion; the former begets
knowledge, the latter ignorance.

Hypocrates
460 – 400 B.C.

The most honest answer to this question is we simply do
not know. Although theories abound, the cause of attention
deficit disorder is still wrapped in mystery. There are many

who believe that attention deficit disorder is a behavioral disorder with its cause in the child's psychosocial environment. They argue that medical practitioners, in collusion with drug companies and some teachers, have *medicalized* the disorder. There is no question that a chaotic home environment, marital discord, mental illness in the family, and many other stress producing situations can cause behavior problems in children. Neither is there any doubt that overcrowded classrooms, staffed by inadequately trained teachers, or boredom in a bright child, as well as a number of other psychosocial factors can also be the cause of hyperactive behavior in some children. On the other hand, one must not hasten to blame psychosocial factors as the sole cause of the child's misbehavior; since an extremely hyperactive child can create chaos both at home and in school, bring out the worst in the family, and interfere with the teaching effectiveness of even the most capable teacher.

Based on our present knowledge, it appears that attention deficit hyperactivity disorder most likely has many causes and that in many hyperactive children varying degrees of psychosocial and biological factors may be operative at the same time. What follows is a brief description of suspected causes of ADHD.

Brain Damage

The notion of a structural abnormality or brain damage as the cause of hyperactivity is still popular particularly in nonscientific circles. Certainly, damage to the brain can cause behavioral changes consistent with the diagnosis of ADHD. However, in the vast majority of cases of hyperactivity, there is neither a history of prenatal injury to the fetus, nor of birth trauma, head injury or brain infection. Compared with nonhyperactive children, however, there is more frequently a history of maternal toxemia during pregnancy, complications of labor, or difficult births.

Head trauma is quite common in childhood, but it is nearly always impossible to relate it to the development of hyperactive behavior. A careful history may reveal that the child had some or all of the behavioral traits associated with hyperactivity before the head injury. In fact, it is quite likely that the impulsive behavior of the hyperactive child may have led to his head trauma in the first place.

Repeated, careful, and detailed neurological examinations of hyperactive children very seldom reveal signs of significant neurological abnormalities. The so-called minor or soft neurological signs such as poor gross or fine motor co-ordination problems that one often sees in some hyperactive children are difficult to interpret since the same signs are also seen in many otherwise normal, non-hyperactive children. Electroencephalogram (EEG or brain wave recording), brain scan, and skull x-rays have never shown findings which would be diagnostically specific for ADHD. It is doubtful that newer diagnostic tools such as magnetic resonance imaging (MRI) or positron emission tomography (PET) will be of value either in delineating the cause of or in diagnosing ADHD. What is certain is that with the increasing appearance in the popular press of articles about these technological advances, there will be a corresponding demand from some parents, encouraged by their neighbors, friends, and some professionals that their children be given the benefit of investigation by these modern tools.

Biochemical Brain Malfunctions

Functional deficiences of various parts of the brain have also been suspected of causing attention deficit disorder. The cause of these deficiencies is not known. There is, however, a great deal of clinical and research evidence pointing to the important role of certain chemical substances produced by the brain, the so-called neurotransmitters, in the genesis of ADHD. In particular an underproduction or an altered function of one of these neurotransmitters, dopamine, is believed to be responsible for the behavioral traits of hyperactive children.

Genetic Influences

There is a significant body of evidence suggesting that genetic factors play a major role in the development of ADHD. This evidence includes the following:

1. There is an increased incidence of reported histories of hyperactivity amongst the parents and relatives of hyperactive children as compared to the parents and relatives of non-hyperactive children.
2. There is an increase in reported cases of hyperactivity among the full siblings of hyperactive children as compared to their half siblings.
3. Many more boys than girls are affected by hyperactivity and this suggests a genetic predisposition in boys.
4. Studies on the occurrence of hyperactivity in twins have demonstrated that when one of the twins is hyperactive, the likelihood of hyperactivity in the other twin is greater if the twins are identical (monozygotic) than if they are non-identical (dizygotic).

Maturational Lag

Since the behavior of hyperactive children is abnormal relative to their own age, but resembles the behavior of normal children of younger ages, it has been suggested that hyperactive children are slow in their development of certain functions of their brains. The problem with this assumption is that a "lag" suggests that eventually these children will "catch-up." Unfortunately, some of the abnormal behavior of a significant number of hyperactive children persists, although less severely, into adulthood. Another problem with the notion of a lag is that it will encourage some professionals and parents to postpone effective treatment of the child, hoping that his brain will eventually mature. During the intervening period, however, the child and his family continue to suffer.

Poisons

Environmental poisons such as lead and other toxic metals have been implicated, but not proven, to cause ADHD. It has been suggested that chronic exposure to lead or other toxic metals at concentrations too low to produce overt clinical signs of poisoning may lead to subtle biochemical changes within the brain and to subsequent development of ADHD symptoms in some children. Up to the present time, we have no definitive evidence of such subtle poisonings.

Smoking and alcohol consumption during pregnancy have also been suspected to cause ADHD. We know that heavy alcohol consumption during pregnancy can lead to the development of Fetal Alcohol Syndrome. This syndrome consists of variable degrees of mental retardation, moderate growth deficiency, abnormal facial structures, and a number of other abnormalities. We also know that babies born to smoking mothers are, on the whole, smaller than babies born to non-smokers. We do not know the possible subtle effects of minimal to moderate alcohol consumption or smoking on the developing fetus. As long as this is not known, it is only prudent for pregnant women to refrain from drinking alcoholic beverages and smoking.

Sensitivity to Fluorescent Light

Fluorescent light has been suggested as a possible cause of hyperactivity in some sensitive individuals. Carefully designed experiments, however, have demonstrated conclusively that this is not true.

Food Sensitivity

The relationship between food and ADHD is discussed in Chapter 10.

How all these possible causative factors might lead to the behavioral patterns observed in ADHD children is not known. There are two theories which attempt to explain how this might take place. One postulates that the brain of ADHD children is overaroused and the other postulates an underarousal of their brains. There is a great deal of laboratory evidence suggesting that dopamine deficiency leads to an underarousal of the brain in ADHD children, making it difficult for them to focus on the important central stimulus and ignore the many irrelevant stimuli which enter their brains at the same time. They pay equal attention to everything around them rather than focusing their attention selectively. Stimulant drugs increase the concentration of dopamine within certain areas of their brains and this in turn results in an elevation of their arousal level and an increase in their ability to focus their attention selectively. In this respect, stimulant drugs behave as they do in normal individuals and do not evoke a contradictory response in ADHD children.

It is interesting to note that Dr. C. Bradley, the originator of stimulant therapy in 1937, came to the same conclusion without knowing anything about dopamine or the underarousal theory. He suggested that since certain parts of the brain have an inhibitory function over stimuli received by the brain through the peripheral nervous system, any stimulation of these parts would enhance their inhibitory function.* He then suggested that this inhibitory function is impaired in hyperactive children and is restored by the action of stimulant drugs.

---

*The following example may serve to explain the concept of inhibitory functions of the brain for those who are not familiar with it. At all times our brain receives continuously and simultaneously multiple stimuli through our senses. We hear sounds, see objects, smell odors, and feel our clothing at the same time. Our brain is, however, programmed to inhibit and ignore irrelevant stimuli and concentrate on the important central stimulus. For example while reading we may also hear people talk or feel the chair we sit on. But subconsciously we ignore everything except the visual stimulus, the written words. This inhibition of irrelevant stimuli is an important part of our brain function. Without it we would be distracted by every sound, sight, and smell, unable to concentrate on what we intend to do.

5

How is ADHD Diagnosed?

A thorough diagnostic evaluation of ADHD requires the input of a team of professionals consisting of a specially trained physician, the child's teacher or a special education teacher, a psychologist, a social worker and possibly other professionals. Such teams are normally available only in certain hospital-based clinics. In the majority of cases, the parents must rely on the family physician to make a diagnosis in cooperation with the child's teacher.

Due to the fact that physicians have no precise way of

measuring inattention, impulsivity, and hyperactivity, the diagnosis of attention deficit disorder remains a relatively difficult task for them. Purposeless overactivity, in particular, is very difficult to measure objectively. A certain amount of activity is quite normal for a three-year-old. However, the same amount of activity is regarded as excessive for an eight-year-old. There are no standardized norms of activity, similar to those of height and weight, against which one can measure the child's activity level. A cynic once defined hyperactivity as the amount of activity which annoys the observer! Although there are some objective tests available for measuring impulsivity and inattention, there are still some difficulties associated with their precise measurement and definition.

The difficulties associated with this lack of precise definition have hampered studies of hyperactivity for a considerable time. Researchers did not have a uniform and precise system of including children in, or excluding them from, their studies. The diagnostic criteria introduced by the American Psychiatric Association in 1981 and revised in 1987 provided the scientists with an additional tool to help them with the clinical diagnosis of attention deficit disorder. Both 1981 and 1987 versions of the diagnostic criteria include guidelines for the exclusion of children with other disorders which may also be associated with hyperactivity or inattention.

Diagnostic criteria for Attention-deficit Hyperactivity Disorder

(Diagnostic and Statistical Manual of Mental Disorders, American Psychiatric Association, 1987 DSM III {R}).

Note: Consider a criterion met only if the behavior is considerably more frequent than that of most people of the same mental age.*
*Note the lack of objectivity in this statement: How frequent is considerably more frequent?

A. A disturbance of at least six months during which at least eight of the following are present:

(1) often fidgets with hands or feet or squirms in seat (in adolescents, may be limited to subjective feelings of restlessness)

(2)   has difficulty remaining seated when required to do so

(3)   is easily distracted by extraneous stimuli

(4)   has difficulty awaiting turn in games or group situations

(5)   often blurts out answers to questions before they have been completed

(6)   has difficulty following through on instructions from others (not due to oppositional behavior or failure of comprehension), e.g. fails to finish chores

(7)   has difficulty sustaining attention in tasks or play activities

(8)   often shifts from one uncompleted activity to another

(9)   has difficulty playing quietly

(10) often talks excessively

(11) often interrupts or intrudes on others, e.g. butts into other children's games

(12) often does not seem to listen to what is being said to him or her

(13) often loses things necessary for tasks or activities at school or at home (e.g. toys, pencils, books, assignments)

(14) often engages in physically dangerous activities without considering possible consequences (not for the purpose of thrill-seeking), e.g. runs into street without looking

Note: The above items are listed in descending order of discriminating power based on data from a national field trial of the DSM-III-R criteria for Disruptive Behavior Disorders.

B. Onset before the age of seven.

C. Does not meet the criteria for a Pervasive Developmental Disorder.

Criteria for severity of Attention-deficit Hyperactivity Disorder:

Mild: Few, if any, symptoms in excess of those required to make the diagnosis and only minimal or no impairment in school and social functioning.

Moderate: Symptoms or functional impairment intermediate between "mild" and "severe."

Severe: Many symptoms in excess of those required to make the diagnosis and significant pervasive impairment in functioning at home and school and with peers.

Although both versions of the diagnostic criteria still contain a great deal of subjectivity, they provide us with a standard format for taking a *history* of hyperactivity, inattention, and impulsivity. Everyone who has consulted a physician knows that an accurate history of an illness, along with a medical examination and laboratory investigations, constitute the essential elements of the diagnosis of that illness.

History

Since the behavior of ADHD children varies from situation to situation (classroom versus physician's office) and from day to day in the same situation, it is important for the professionals to observe the child and to obtain behavioral reports from his parents and teachers. Inconsistency of behavior is a characteristic of ADHD children. In the one-to-one situation of the physician's office such children often behave very normally. The teachers and parents of the same children, however, usually report completely different behavior patterns. Experienced professionals rely heavily on these reports, since both teachers and parents have observed the child over a longer period of time and have had the opportunity to compare him with other children of the same age.

There are many standardized parent-teacher questionnaires for the purpose of obtaining information on child behavior. Perhaps the most well-known of these is the Conners' Parent-Teacher questionnaire. The abbreviated forms of this questionnaire are very commonly used by many hospital-based clinics and physicians in private practice. A modified version of it is used at our clinic. Information obtained from the behavior-rating questionnaires is supplemented by the history of the child and is used to ascertain whether the child meets the diagnostic criteria developed by the American Psychiatric Association.

Parent Questionnaire

Child's Name: _____

INSTRUCTIONS: Listed below are items concerning children's behavior or the problems they sometimes have. Read each item carefully and decide how much you think this child has been displaying this behavior **today.**

Today's Date: _____   Day No. _____
                    Month Day Year

Parent's Name: _____

Observation	Frequency (Check one only)			
	Not at All	Just a Little	Often	Almost Always
1. Body in constant motion.	[ ]	[ ]	[ ]	[ ]
2. Difficulty sitting through a meal.	[ ]	[ ]	[ ]	[ ]
3. Constant squirming while watching TV or playing with toys.	[ ]	[ ]	[ ]	[ ]
4. Restless in the car, church, while shopping, etc.	[ ]	[ ]	[ ]	[ ]
5. Keeps changing activities or games.	[ ]	[ ]	[ ]	[ ]
6. Starts things without finishing them; does not complete tasks.	[ ]	[ ]	[ ]	[ ]
7. Difficulty playing cooperatively with others for more than a few minutes.	[ ]	[ ]	[ ]	[ ]
8. Does not seem to listen attentively or hear what you say.	[ ]	[ ]	[ ]	[ ]
9. Stares at things for long periods.	[ ]	[ ]	[ ]	[ ]
10. Talks too much or too loudly.	[ ]	[ ]	[ ]	[ ]
11. Interrupts or interferes with other's conversations or activities.	[ ]	[ ]	[ ]	[ ]
12. Mood changes quickly and unpredictably.	[ ]	[ ]	[ ]	[ ]
13. Easily frustrated; demands must be met immediately.	[ ]	[ ]	[ ]	[ ]
14. Acts without thinking.	[ ]	[ ]	[ ]	[ ]

Comments: _____

_____

_____

_____

Teacher Questionnaire

Child's Name: _____

Instructions: Listed below are items concerning children's behavior or the problems they sometimes have. Read each item carefully and decide how much you think this child has been displaying this behavior **today.**

Today's Date: _____   Day No. _____
          Month   Day   Year

Teacher's Name: _____

Observation	Frequency (Check one only)			
	Not at All	Just a Little	Often	Almost Always
1. Difficulty sitting still or excessive fidgeting, restlessness.	[ ] [ ]	[ ] [ ]	[ ] [ ]	[ ] [ ]
2. Difficulty staying seated, often on the go.	[ ]	[ ]	[ ]	[ ]
3. Starts things without finishing them; does not complete tasks.	[ ] [ ]	[ ] [ ]	[ ] [ ]	[ ] [ ]
4. Doesn't seem to listen attentively when spoken to.	[ ]	[ ]	[ ]	[ ]
5. Has difficulty following oral directions.	[ ]	[ ]	[ ]	[ ]
6. Easily distracted, difficulty concentrating	[ ]	[ ]	[ ]	[ ]
7. Difficulty staying with a play activity.	[ ]	[ ]	[ ]	[ ]
8. Acts before thinking.	[ ]	[ ]	[ ]	[ ]
9. Has difficulty organizing work.	[ ]	[ ]	[ ]	[ ]
10. Needs a lot of supervision.	[ ]	[ ]	[ ]	[ ]
11. Interacts poorly with other children.	[ ]	[ ]	[ ]	[ ]
12. Demands must be met immediately, easily frustrated.	[ ]	[ ]	[ ]	[ ]
13. Mood changes quickly, cries, temper outbursts.	[ ]	[ ]	[ ]	[ ]

Comments: _____

_____

_____

_____

It is important to realize that the process of diagnosis is not complete unless other disorders with similar patterns of behavior are ruled out. To do this, additional information must be obtained through a detailed interview of the parents. This usually includes the following:

- The onset, severity and frequency of the troublesome behaviors and their possible precipitating factors.
- The history of mental health problems or childhood hyperactivity in the parents and their siblings as well as in the child's siblings.
- The number of children in the family and the amount and severity of sibling rivalry.
- The presence of marital discord and other family stressors.
- How the family is coping with the ADHD child and what supports are available to them in the community.
- The consistency of parental disciplinary measures and the child's response to them.
- Maternal health problems during pregnancy and the events associated with labor, delivery and the early days of life.
- Feeding and sleeping problems in the child during infancy.
- Medications that the child may be taking.

This type of careful and detailed history helps us to differentiate between ADHD and other disruptive behavior disorders which have similar patterns of behavior, but require a different type of treatment. It also helps us to differentiate a child suffering from ADHD from a learning-disabled child who has become frustrated with his inability to cope with the demands of school and has consequently developed fidgetiness, inattention and disruptive behavior. The learning-disabled child usually does not have a history of behavior problems in preschool years and his abnormal behavior is not apparent outside of school. It is important to re-emphasize that some children may suffer from ADHD, other behavioral disorders, and a learning disorder at the same time. In such cases, each aspect of their problem must receive appropriate treatment. A learning-disabled child who is also suffering from ADHD may require special education, stimulant therapy and, if necessary, behavior therapy. His family may also require supportive counselling.

Commonly Reported Behavior Patterns:

As mentioned previously, the behavior of ADHD children changes with age and maturation. Furthermore, ADHD children do not always exhibit the full repertoire of abnormal behaviors which are commonly reported for their age. Appropriate treatment also modifies their behavior to various extents. What follows is a brief presentation of commonly *reported* behaviors of ADHD children. It is important to know that carefully designed research studies have demonstrated that some of these reported behaviors do not, in fact, occur more frequently in ADHD children than they do in non-ADHD children.

In infancy, hyperactivity is usually the only noticeable feature. It is often present in the first year of life. The baby may be constantly wiggling and difficult to hold. Some mothers report excessive motor activity even before the child is born. In this stage of the child's development, his hyperactivity is not usually bothersome. His parents are usually more troubled by his disturbed pattern of feeding and sleeping. The child is often a poor feeder and is colicky. Colic in non-hyperactive children usually disappears by three or four months of age. In hyperactive children, however, it may be present during the entire first year of life. During this time, the hyperactive child may demand constant attention by fussing and crying. He seems to need constant entertainment. He may also have a difficult time falling asleep and may wake up frequently during the night. This may continue long beyond the age when most children begin to sleep through the night, that is, three to four months of age. After the child starts to crawl or walk, his hyperactivity and curiosity make him a first class explorer.

This usually leads to more than his share of accidents through such activities as climbing up and falling from furniture and crawling under the kitchen sink to help himself to detergents, solvents, bleach, or whatever else he can find. He seems to have several busy hands and is usually several steps ahead of his parents. Of course in this age group, no one expects any child to be attentive and impulsivity, that is, acting without much thinking is quite normal.

During the preschool years the excessive motor activity persists and may become even more prominent. Difficulties with attention and impulse control, however, become more evident now. The child seems to go from activity to activity and, unless his parents or his play school teacher stand next to him, he will not remain with any activity for more than a very short period of time. He grabs toys from other children, disrupting their play, and may show aggression towards them, and may disrupt their play. He manages to become very unpopular with other children because he always wants to have his own way. He can learn the rules of good behavior, but somehow seems to be unable to follow these rules unless he is constantly reminded. Punishment of any sort does not seem to have any effect on him. His impulsivity continues, as does his accident proneness. He may dash across the street without looking, or get himself fearlessly into dangerous situations. Sleep difficulties may continue during this age. He may wake up in the middle of the night to raid the refrigerator, turn the television on, or otherwise explore the household, wondering why everyone else is asleep. Some hyperactive children are also early risers and often are not in a happy mood when they wake up. Mood swings and temper outbursts may become apparent in this age.

In early school years the most troublesome problem for the child is his poor ability to attend to learning tasks. Usually he has the ability to learn, but he cannot attend long enough to do so. He starts tasks but leaves them incomplete, because he is distracted by everything around him. Consequently, he falls behind in his school work. If he is very bright, however, he may learn in spite of his poor ability to attend. Hyperactivity, in terms of excessive walking around the classroom, may or may not be present. More often, however, he is fidgity and constantly squirming. He talks loudly and out of turn and generally disrupts the class. He tends to answer the questions before the teacher has finished the sentence, that is, if he is not daydreaming. His teacher reports that often he seems to be in a different world. He is disorganized and his work is usually quite messy. His disregard for rules continues, and he is often left out of organized games. He may feel rejected and lonely, thus his self-esteem begins to suffer. His disturbed sleep pattern continues, and he may now have nightmares. His mood swings may also continue, and his low level of tolerance for frustration will lead to increased temper outbursts and aggression towards his peers, parents and teacher.

After the child has reached ten or eleven years of age, his hyperactivity often becomes less noticeable, although he may still be fidgity and restless. During this period, his poor impulse control severely interferes with his social interaction. His socialization skills are poor, awkward, and counterproductive. He may be craving friendship, but becomes more isolated and may engage in antisocial behavior. His social and academic failure may lead to depression and further isolation.

Inattention and impulsivity may continue into adulthood. The young adult may still be restless, although hyperactivity usually has disappeared.

Medical Examination

Children of school age are often brought to the physicians at the request of their teachers. Not infrequently, the parents report that the child's teacher has recommended a neurological examination for the child, including an electroencephalogram (brain wave recording). Occasionally, the parents also ask for a brain scan or for some other expensive tests.

It is the experience of all physicians who have worked with hyperactive and learning-disabled children that medical examination and routine blood and urine tests in these children almost invariably produce normal results. Likewise, detailed neurological examination of these children usually reveals no significant abnormalities.

Not infrequently, one finds ADHD children who show slight delays in the maturation of their nervous system such as a poor ability to balance on one foot, hop, or to move hands back and forth rapidly. They may also have difficulties knowing the right and left sides of their own body. These so-called soft neurological signs, however, are seen also in many children who have no attention or learning problems. Minor variations in electroencephalograms are seen in many ADHD as well as normal children. Electroencephalograms are of no value in the diagnosis of ADHD, but they are most useful if there is any suggestion that the child may have a seizure problem.*

This, of course, does not mean that a medical examination is totally useless. The experienced physician knows that a good and complete medical examination, including an assessment of the child's hearing and vision, is essential for ruling out any possible physical problems and assures the parents that the physician is thorough and interested in making sure that everything is done to come to a proper diagnosis. This, in turn, increases the parents' confidence and trust in their physician and will lead to a better working relationship and compliance with any recommended treatment. It should also reduce "doctor shopping," particularly where insured medical services are available, and the parents do not have any out-of-pocket expenditures in seeking medical care. All told, there are no specific and characteristic medical, neurological, or laboratory tests which can be used for making a reliable diagnosis of ADHD. The history provides us with the most useful diagnostic clues.

---

*Promising new developments in neurometrics through computer–assisted quantitative analysis of electroencephalograms are available. Some investigators claim that these techniques enable us to differentiate between those learning and behavior disorders which are caused by brain dysfunction and those of environmental origin. The usefulness of the day–to–day clinical application of these techniques in the diagnosis of these disorders is still controversial.

Psychological Tests

There are a number of psychological tests which provide us with very useful information for making the diagnosis of ADHD. Taken together with the history of the child's problem, these tests enable us to make a diagnosis of ADHD with a relatively high degree of reliability.

The most commonly used test of intelligence in schools is the revised Wechsler Intelligence Scales for Children (WISC-R). This test has a number of subtests (arithmetic, coding, information, and digit span) which require the child to focus and sustain his attention on test items. ADHD children often score low in these subtests because of their characteristically low resistance to distraction.

There are other tests which attempt to measure the child's selective and sustained attention; these include the Paired Associate Learning Test and the Continuous Performance Test. These tests of vigilance have been criticized for their inability to differentiate between a child who is not motivated (application deficit) and a child who is unable to focus his attention (attention deficit).

Another useful test is the so-called Matching Familiar Figures Test (MFFT). The child is asked to look at a figure and then identify the same figure among a number of other similar, but slightly different, figures. The impulsive child often has a very short "latency period," that is, quickly and without looking carefully, he points to a figure which may or may not be correct. He does not take time to think, consequently he makes more mistakes than non- ADHD children.

These and similar psychological tests are also available for preschool children. Interested teachers should consult their school psychologist for more information about psychological tests which may be useful for the diagnosis of ADHD.

Since many ADHD children have associated academic difficulties, certain educational tests also provide very useful information, particularly in helping to differentiate between ADHD children and those who are learning-disabled and have become inattentive as a result of their inability to cope with their academic difficulties.

Hair Analysis

Occasionally, parents ask for a hair analysis of their children to diagnose potential poisoning with lead or other toxic substances. Many commercial laboratories offer hair analysis services, and often they give the results of their tests in impressive computer print-outs. Unfortunately, commercial hair analysis has not proven to be a reliable test for this purpose. A sample of a child's hair, divided in two parts, and sent simultaneously to the same commercial laboratory under two different fictitious names, produced two completely different results for one of us (HM). Even if hair analysis were reliable and accurate, its results would not necessarily reflect the status of the tested elements in the child's brain or elsewhere in his body. Better tests for detecting environmental toxins in blood and urine are available to the child's physician, and can be ordered if the child's history and medical examination warrant such tests.

Allergy Tests

Some parents ask for allergy tests for their hyperactive children. There is no clearcut evidence that allergy plays a role in ADHD. Such tests have been very unproductive up to the present time. No one has ever demonstrated a convincing cause-and-effect relationship between allergy and ADHD, similar to those existing between pollens and hayfever or peanuts and hives. There is, however, some evidence that immunological disorders (including allergies) are seen more frequently in learning disabled and ADHD children than in normal childhood population. The relationship between food and hyperactivity will be discussed in Chapter 10.

In summary, the diagnosis of ADHD requires careful attention to the history of the child, obtained through interviewing the parents, and when applicable, the child, and supplemented by reviewing the behavior rating questionnaires completed by his parents and teachers. This history together with the observation of the child and, when necessary, the administration of a number of psychological and educational tests, can usually provide significant information for the diagnosis of ADHD. Unfortunately, there is no single or simple test to help us make a definitive diagnosis of ADHD.

6

How is ADHD Treated?

Healing is a matter of time, but it is also sometimes a matter of opportunity.

Hypocrates
460 – 400 B.C.

The aim of treatment of any disorder is either to cure it, or to improve the affected individual's sense of well–being. When the cause of a disorder is known, the treatment aim is, whenever possible, to eliminate it and to cure the disorder. However, when the cause of a disorder is not known, treatment measures are usually directed toward an amelioration of its disturbing symptoms. Such is the case with the treatment of ADHD. At the present time, there is no known cure for it. The aim of the treatment is to improve the child's socialization skills by enabling him to control his impulsive behavior, and to better his school performance by improving the quality and span of his attention. This improvement in the child's socialization skills and school performance should then lead to an enhanced sense of self- esteem. An important by-product of the treatment is, of course, a reduction in the child's amount of purposeless movements and activities. Many children with ADHD improve with maturation and some of them even "outgrow" their problems. All of them, however, will suffer needlessly during their maturation, if they are not given the benefit of the presently available treatment.

In this chapter we will discuss the medical approaches to

the treatment of ADHD. The following chapters will deal with the equally important behavior management of ADHD children at home and in school. At the outset, it must be said that every treatment approach has its advocates. The preponderance of evidence from research, indicates that, at the present time, stimulant drugs are the most effective form of treatment available for most children with ADHD. Ideally, a treatment program should include stimulant drugs, behavior management, family counselling, and a modified education program.

Stimulant Therapy

In spite of the clearly-demonstrated effectiveness of stimulant drugs in the treatment of hyperactive children, one can justifiably ask why these children should be given drugs for a behavior disorder. The answer to this question lies in our understanding of the main manifestations of ADHD. Hyperactive children have a difficult time concentrating and focusing their attention long enough on a task to complete it. They are distracted by what they hear, see, and feel; even by their own thoughts. They are impulsive; they act before thinking and planning their actions. They need help to focus their attention and to pause and plan their actions. Stimulants enable them to do so. The aim of the treatment is not to drug them to submission or to convert them to zombies. On the contrary, the purpose of stimulant therapy is to give hyperactive children control over their own actions and behavior, to enable them to think about the consequences of their behavior, and to assist them to be attentive and goal-oriented. In essence, stimulants help them to liberate themselves from imprisonment in their disorder.

Many physicians prefer to combine the medical treatment with a behavioral management program for the child. Some physicians even go as far as refusing to prescribe medications, if no appropriate behavioral/educational modification for the child is instituted at the same time. The combined approach appears to produce the best results. Since most family physicians and many pediatricians are neither qualified in developing a behavior management program, nor have sufficient time to do this, they must seek the assistance of other professionals to develop such a program for the child. To be effective, a behavior management program must be consistent at home and in school. This will be further discussed in the following chapters.

Since the aim of stimulant therapy is to improve the child's behavior and academic performance, the best results will be achieved through a coordinated effort of the child's physician, parents and teachers. The important role that the child's teacher plays in helping to make the diagnosis is surpassed only by their active involvement in treating the child. The child's teacher is in an important position to know if stimulant therapy is effective, much more so than the prescribing physician. Periodic contacts between the child's physician and his teacher make it possible for the physician to modify the child's treatment program based on his response during school hours.

Which children will benefit from stimulant therapy?

The majority of ADHD children, if properly diagnosed, will respond favorably to stimulant therapy. A few children, however, either do not respond at all, or show an adverse response. We have no means of knowing in advance how children may respond to stimulant drugs, since there are no predictive specific signs or symptoms. The history of the child, however, provides the trained physician with sufficient information to enable him to conclude which child is *most likely* to respond favorably to stimulant drugs. If the child has had symptoms of ADHD long before entering school and his symptoms are present, in varying degrees, in all situations, he is likely to benefit from stimulant therapy. As previously discussed, many children with ADHD also suffer simultaneously from other conditions such as learning disabilities. Others are, at the same time, victims of psychosocial influences such as poorly-functioning families. These simultaneously-occuring conditions may lead the child's physician away from the diagnosis of ADHD and the usefulness of medications. The only way to know a child's response to stimulant therapy is to try it. It is good practice to try stimulant therapy, so that no child who might benefit from it will be denied these benefits. It is, however, not a good practice to prescribe drugs without adequate diagnosis and without assessing the child's response to the medication.

Drug trials can also be used as a diagnostic tool, even though a favorable response to the medication does not necessarily confirm the diagnosis of ADHD. This is because stimulant drugs also improve the awareness and attention span of normal individuals. Also, many research studies have demonstrated the placebo effect of the drug therapy. The placebo effect is noted when the child's parents and/or teacher perceive an improvement in his behavior, even though he is not receiving a stimulant drug. For this reason, many hospital-based clinics and some physicians in private practice resort to what is known as a blind trial of medication. In this type of trial, a pharmacist provides the child's parents with individually packed pills or capsules which may be either a stimulant drug or an ineffective substance, a placebo. The pills or capsules look exactly the same. The pharmacist knows which day the child receives a drug and which day a placebo; but the child, his physician, parents, and teacher do not know this until the end of the trial. They are "blind" to it.

There are a number of ways that drug trials can be carried out, and each physician has his own preference. In all cases, the teachers and the parents are asked to complete, either daily or weekly, behavior rating questionnaires. If the child's behavior is improved significantly and consistently on medication days as compared to placebo days, he is considered to be a favorable responder. Otherwise, the medication is discontinued or another medication is tried. A significant improvement is usually defined as at least a 20% improvement in behavior ratings of the child by his teacher and/or parents. The questionnaires are designed for easy quantification in terms of numerical values. Many physicians attach a greater significance to the teacher's ratings than to the parent's ratings, because the child is normally with his teacher during the hours that the drug is most effective. If the drug trial continues during the weekend, the parents have, of course, a similar opportunity to observe the child's behavior during the peak hours of drug effectiveness. This will be discussed further in the following pages. Drug trials should never be attempted during the summer months when the teacher's input is not available.

Some physicians vary the dose of medication and placebo during the course of the trial in order to establish the most effective drug dose for the child. Others use a fixed dose during the trial, and if the child responds favorably to stimulant therapy, they attempt to adjust the medication dose following the trial.

What drugs are available for the treatment of ADHD?

The most commonly used drug is *methylphenidate* which is best known by its brand name Ritalin. It is a relatively short-acting stimulant drug with some appetite suppressing properties. After ingestion, a change in the child's behavior is noticed in about one hour, the peak effectiveness is reached between two and three hours, and four hours after ingestion most children revert to their usual behavior. Most of the drug is discharged from the child's body by that time. If the child receives his first dose in the morning, he may require a second dose at noon in order to carry him through the school day. Older children may require a third dose late in the afternoon. Ritalin is also available in a sustained-release form which, the manufacturer claims, is effective over a longer period of time and eliminates the necessity of a noon dose. Clinical experience, however, shows that for many children the sustained-release form of Ritalin is not as effective as the regular form, given in two or three doses through the day. *Methylphenidate* is available also in a non- brand form in some countries and probably is less expensive in this form.

Another commonly prescribed drug is *pemoline* which is marketed under its brand name Cylert. It is a long-acting stimulant drug which enables the child to take only a morning dose. It is, however, somewhat difficult to adjust the dose of *pemoline* and, for this and other reasons, it has not been as popular as *methylphenidate* with many physicians. Its appetite suppressing properties are less pronounced than Ritalin.

Another stimulant drug which is effective in treating ADHD children is *dextroamphetamine,* available under its brand name Dexedrine. It is very similar to *methylphenidate* in its action, and it is also available in a slow release form. It is a more potent appetite suppresser than Ritalin or Cylert.

Occasionally, some physicians prescribe other drugs such as an antidepressant–Trofranil, or a tranquilizer–Mellaril. These drugs have not been as widely studied as stimulant drugs in the treatment of ADHD, and many physicians shy away from their use because of their undesirable side effects when used over prolonged periods of time.

Other drugs which are occasionally used for the treatment of hyperactivity are Benadryl, an antihistamine and Atarax, a mild tranquilizer. Their effectiveness in the treatment of ADHD has not been proven. Sedatives such as *phenobarbital* are ineffective in the treatment of ADHD children and often lead to a deterioration of their behavior.

How safe are the drugs used for the treatment of ADHD?

Methylphenidate and *amphetamines* have been used for several decades and have proven remarkably safe and effective in their usual doses for the vast majority of children. There are some individuals, however, who show adverse responses to these medications such as skin rashes, or hives, much the same way as some other individuals respond to eating peanuts or shellfish. These are individual sensitivities and must be reported to the child's physician as soon as they are noted.

Although *pemoline* has been in the market also for quite a number of years, it has not been as widely studied as other stimulant drugs. It has adverse effects similar to other stimulant drugs in some children. In our experience stimulant drugs do not cause short stature and do not have undesirable long term side effects (see section on side effects).

There are a number of medical reasons why stimulant drugs should not be used for some children with ADHD. These include pre- existing conditions such as seizures, severe depression, high blood pressure, chronic liver or kidney disease, Tourette's Syndrome, etc. The prescribing physician will know these and other contraindications.

How do stimulant drugs work?

Some research studies suggest that stimulant drugs increase the concentration of dopamine within the brain, and, in doing so, enable the child to gain control over his behavior, to pay attention to the most important stimulus entering his brain, to concentrate on the task at hand, and to filter out all irrelevant stimuli.

As mentioned previously, some clinicians believe that the core problem of ADHD children may not be an attention deficit but an application deficit, that is, they consciously choose not to pay attention. Whether stimulant drugs improve the child's attention so that he can allocate his cognitive resources to a task, or improve his attitude so that he applies himself and does what he is capable of doing, is irrelevant. The fact is that stimulant drugs work in about 70% to 75% of ADHD children. Their teachers and parents see an improvement in their attitude, behavior, and work habits. The child becomes more available to instruction and thus, easier to teach. These changes in the child seem to result from his enhanced arousal state and his increased ability to focus his attention.

When a child with ADHD does not respond to the usual doses of stimulant drugs, one should question the accuracy of the initial diagnosis and look for other causes to explain his behavior. These children may be good candidates for behavior therapy and their families may benefit from supportive counselling. Some children who respond adversely to a stimulant drug during the initial trial may respond favorably to smaller doses of the same drug or a different stimulant drug.

A number of years ago, some investigators suggested that learning in ADHD children improves only as long as they are taking stimulant drugs. It was feared that children would forget what they had learned when they discontinued taking their medication (state- dependent learning.) Later research did not substantiate these concerns.

What is the best dose of stimulant drugs?

ADHD children are a very heterogeneous group of individuals and their response to medication varies greatly. On the whole, the younger the child, the smaller the required dose to achieve the desired effect. Normally, the stimulant drugs are not prescribed for children under 5 or 6 years of age. The manufacturers of Ritalin and Cylert do not recommend their use for children under 6 years of age and the manufacturer of Dexedrine does not recommend its use for children under 3 years of age.

Some research studies indicate that the lower doses of stimulant drugs improve the child's attention span and the quality of his academic performance; somewhat higher doses improve his impulse control and consequently his social interactions. The higher doses, according to these investigators, may have even a slightly deleterious effect on the child's academic performance. Other research studies, however, contradict this finding and suggest no differential effect on behavior and attention. The dose of stimulant drugs must be adjusted for each child, in order to obtain the most desirable response.

Many physicians start with a small dose based on the child's weight, and increase the dose gradually until, according to the child's teacher and parents, the best results are obtained. Other physicians start with a fixed average dose of, say, one pill in the morning and one at noon, and obtain feedback from the child's teacher and parents in order to adjust the dose, if necessary. Some physicians find it more appropriate to discuss with the parents the rationale for stimulant therapy, the effects and side effects of the drug, and the signs and symptoms of overdosing the child. They then instruct the parents to increase or decrease the dose within certain limits, say, a maximum of four pills per day, until optimal results are obtained. It is never wise to change the dose of medication without first consulting the physician who prescribed the medication.

As the child grows older, the dose may have to be increased in order to maintain the same level of beneficial results. Some children with poor socialization skills may require a higher dose of stimulant medication after 10 or 11 years of age. Older children may need smaller doses as they go through the maturation process.

When should the drug be taken?

Many physicians prefer to advise that the drug be taken 10 to 20 minutes before breakfast and lunch. They believe that food in the child's stomach interferes with the absorption of the drug. There are a few research studies which indicate that the blood concentration of the drug at various intervals following the ingestion is the same for each interval, whether the drug is taken before or with meals. These investigators, however, caution about generalization of their findings, since their studies were carried out on a small number of individuals.

In our own experience, many parents who discontinued giving medications prescribed by their family physicians because of inconsistent response in their children, report a more favorable and consistent response when instructed to give the child's medications before meals. It is possible that the absorption of stimulant drugs is erratic when taken with meals. On some days the absorption may be rapid, and on other days it may be prolonged. Taking the drug 10 to 20 minutes before meals eliminates this erratic response pattern and, has another beneficial side effect: no reduction of appetite at the next mealtime. If the drug is taken 10 to 20 minutes before breakfast, the child's appetite is rarely affected at lunch time. On the other hand, when it is taken with breakfast, not infrequently the child reports a poor appetite at lunch time. This is most likely due to a slow absorption of the drug when taken with breakfast, which results in its slow elimination. Consequently, a part of stimulant medication is still circulating in the child's blood and interferes with his appetite at lunch time. However, if the drug is taken over 30 minutes before a meal, it can interfere with the child's appetite at that meal time. For these reasons, it is best to adhere to a program of giving the child's medication with a little water 10 to 20 minutes before his meals.

Some older children may require a third dose of medication late in the afternoon if they have school related homework to do or if it is necessary for helping them to control their behavior during the evening hours. In such cases the child's appetite may be depressed during the supper time. Should this happen, the child should be given a nutritious snack before bedtime, in order to maintain his total daily nutrition intake.

How long should the drug be taken?

The simple answer to this question is: As long as the child requires it. The best way to know whether the child continues to benefit from stimulant medications is to discontinue treatment periodically and observe the child's behavior. Many physicians recommend that the child be taken off medication for one to two weeks in the fall, usually several weeks after school has started. It is not a good idea to discontinue medication at the start of the school year for two reasons: First, the beginning of the school year may be full of excitement for the child in a new classroom, with new classmates and a new teacher. Any change in the child's behavior may be due to this excitement rather than the discontinuation of his treatment. Secondly, if a true deterioration in the child's behavior follows the discontinuation of the treatment in the first week of school, he may be labeled as a behavior problem, a label which he may find difficult to shake off.

Temporary discontinuations of the drug should also be

avoided during the weeks when other excitements are imminent such as Thanksgiving or Halloween, birthday parties, and school outings. It is best to discontinue medications without the teacher's knowledge, if this is possible. This is not to be interpreted as an insult to the teacher's intelligence. As human beings, we may all be biased either in favor of or against medications. When we are "blind" to the child's state of medication, we are in a better position to give an unbiased judgement regarding his behavior. At the end of the drug-free period, the child's teacher is asked whether a deterioration in the child's behavior has taken place. As stated previously, the child's teacher is in the best position to know whether stimulant therapy should continue. Of course, the parents' observation during the drug-free time is also very important.

Many children learn strategies to focus and sustain their attention and to increase their impulse control during adolescent years. They may no longer require medications. Others, however, continue to benefit from medication and should be encouraged to take it for as long as they need it. We know, however, that many adolescents dislike taking prescribed drugs because they believe they no longer need them, or because they do not wish to appear different in the eyes of their peers and to be labeled. Unfortunately, those who discontinue their medication are often those who benefit most from it.

There are also a few adults who continue taking stimulant drugs in order to maintain their concentration powers and control their impulses.

Should the stimulant drug be taken continuously?

Many physicians believe that medications should be given only during the school days. They recommend the so-called "drug holidays," discontinuation of the drug on weekends, during the school holidays, and in summer months. Other physicians believe that the child is learning in every situation, whether in school, at home, in a church, on a playground, or in a supermarket, and needs to control his impulses in all situations and at all times. Thus, they recommend that the medication be given every day, much the same way as a diabetic child is given insulin every day.

If stimulant drugs help the child, he should not be expected to supervise his own medication intake. Most children dislike medications of any sort and do their utmost not to take them. They may even keep the pills in their mouth and spit them out whenever they are out of the sight of their parents and teachers. Teenagers, particularly, dislike taking prescribed medications. However, if the medication has been effective in improving their social behavior, they should continue taking it. This may require a great deal of counselling by a trusted physician, parent, or teacher to continue with their treatment. In order to obtain the child's confidence and assure better compliance with the recommended treatment, many physicians find it advantageous to discuss with the child in private the reason for drug therapy and the benefits that he might derive from it. private counselling by a trusted physician, parent, or teacher.

What Are the Side Effects of the Stimulant Drugs?

Stimulant drugs have remarkably few side effects, if they are given in appropriate doses. They do, however, have some short and long term side effects. The most common short term side effects are interference with the child's appetite and sleep. Stimulant drugs suppress appetite. Since, however, they are short-acting, the child's appetite is normal in the vast majority of cases four to five hours after the drug intake. As mentioned previously, this is particularly true if the medication is taken 15 to 30 minutes before breakfast or lunch. If poor appetite persists irrespective of when the drug is taken, either the medication dose should be decreased or the child should be given a nutritious snack before bedtime, to compensate for his reduced food intake during the regular meal times. Very rarely, a child's appetite remains poor even after a reduction in his drug dose. Bedtime snacks are most beneficial for these children.

Interference with sleep is usually not a problem when the child's last dose of daily medication is given at least four to five hours before bedtime. If the child continues to have difficulty falling asleep, his medication dose should be reduced. Occasionally, a child on Cylert may have difficulty falling asleep. If a reduction in the dose of Cylert does not alleviate this problem, or results in a deterioration of his behavior, a change of medication may become necessary.

There are a number of other, rarely reported, short term side effects of stimulant drugs. Most of these side effects are transitory, that is, they disappear in a few days to a few weeks. Many of these so-called side effects have also been reported following treatment with placebos! It is not unusual for the young child to complain of "abdominal pains" or being "sick in the stomach," and for the older child of a "butterfly feeling" in his stomach during the first few days of treatment. Younger children may complain of "headaches," and older children of "light-headedness" or "dizziness."

Infrequently, a child on stimulant therapy becomes depressed and cries easily. Usually a reduction in the dose will promptly eliminate this problem. It should be noted that some parents who have been accustomed to the child's hyperactivity, may interpret his reduced activity level following medication as an abnormal behavior. They may believe that their child has become a zombie, while in fact he has become normal. If the child becomes dazed, listless and lethargic, a reduction in the dose is usually indicated. Otherwise, the parents will become accustomed to the child's reduced level of activity in a few days. Tremors, nervous tics, anxiety, irritability, over-talkativeness, and dry mouth are signs of overdose. If a reduction in the dose does not eliminate these, the medication should be discontinued altogether.

Occasionally, the child's blood pressure and pulse rate increase slightly. Again, a reduction in the dose should bring these back to a normal level. The child's pulse rate, blood pressure, height and weight should be checked, at least every six months.

Clearly, most of the above are not true side effects of medication and can be eliminated with a reduction in dose.

In the early days of stimulant therapy, when the drugs were prescribed more indiscriminately, their most common side effect was an interference with height and weight gain. This interference with the child's growth is very seldom a problem today, as long as the child's total nutrition intake remains adequate for his growth. Some investigators have found changes in the concentration of growth hormone following stimulant therapy. However, most clinicians do not report an interference with height gain and this speaks against any adverse effect of stimulant drugs on growth hormone. In our experience, no child has experienced a reduction in height or weight gain even after several years of stimulant therapy.

Psychological side effects of the drug may be either beneficial or harmful to the child. An improved sense of self-esteem is obviously a plus for the child. However, if the medication reinforces a child's belief that he has no control over his own behavior, and he has to take his pill in order to fight external forces which influence his behavior, he may develop a distorted view of his personal responsibility for his actions. This psychological maladaptation may be reinforced by such remarks by the child's teacher, parents, siblings or peers, such as, "Did you take your pill today?" or "Go and take your pill," whenever he shows a minor behavior deviation. It is the responsibility of physicians, parents, and teachers to emphasize to the child that he is responsible for his own behavior, and that the pill only helps him in his efforts. In the same vein, any improvement in the child's behavior and his interpersonal relationships should be credited to the child and not to to his medication.

One of the beneficial side effects of stimulant drugs is a change in the parents' and teacher's attitude towards the child in response to his improved behavior. Studies have shown that parents become less directive and less critical of their children following stimulant therapy. This positive change of attitude in adults around the child can only be beneficial to the child's sense of self-esteem in the long run.

Stimulant medications should not be given to children with a personal or family history suggestive of Tourette's Syndrome. Tourette's Syndrome is characterized by multiple tics, usually involving face and hands and less frequently arms and legs. Affected individuals often make noises such as grunts, throat clearing, barks, coughs, or use inappropriate words, or obscenities. Presence of multiple tics in a child, even without other symptoms of Tourette's Syndrome, should caution the physician against the use of stimulant drugs which might precipitate this troublesome syndrome.

Are stimulant drugs addictive?

Many years of experience have demonstrated that children receiving stimulant drugs do not develop dependence on or tolerance to these drugs. On the contrary, many of them attempt not to take their medication whenever they can do so, in spite of the fact that they obviously benefit from it.

There are conflicting reports about increased risk of alcohol or other substance abuse among adolescents and adults who were hyperactive in childhood as compared with the general adolescent and adult population. This increased risk appears to be true primarily for a subgroup of hyperactive children who are also aggressive, come from poor socio-economic backgrounds or chaotic home environments, are of lower intelligence, and continue with a lingering poor self-esteem. It should be noted, however, that the increased risk, if any, has been determined from the studies of *groups* of ADHD children. There are no predictive signs which would indicate a poor prognosis for an *individual* child with ADHD. Indeed, it appears very likely that the medication-induced improvement in the child's behavior and self-esteem will decrease his risk of alcohol and drug abuse in later years. At the present time, it is fair to say that so far no clear-cut correlation has been established between the use of stimulant drugs for the treatment of hyperactivity and the later increased or decreased rate of abuse of alcohol and street drugs by hyperactive children. This is further discussed in Chapter 11.

Are stimulant drugs used for preschool children?

Attention deficit disorder, unless associated with extreme hyperactivity, is seldom diagnosed in preschool children and when diagnosed, most physicians prefer not to use stimulant drugs for their treatment. It is felt that, during this stage of their development, unlike their school years when children are expected to conform to the rules of the classroom, their behavior can be modified with behavior management programs designed for use by their parents. As stated previously, most family physicians and many pediatricians have little training in this field. They will be most helpful to the families if they refer them to psychiatrists, clinical psychologists, trained social workers, or, if available, specialized clinics in their communities.

Most parents of hyperactive preschool children are tolerant of their behaviors. Some very hyperactive children, however, disrupt the family life to such an extent that medical intervention may become necessary. These are usually the little tyrants who terrorize the neighborhood, and tax their parents' patience. In such cases, small doses of stimulant drugs are occasionally prescribed by some physicians.

Sedatives such as *phenobarbital* are usually ineffective in the treatment of hyperactive preschool children. Tranquilizers such as Valium or antidepressants such Tofranil are not recommended for the treatment of hyperactivity in preschool children, since they are not safe for prolonged use in this age group. There is probably one exception to this general rule. When the parents cannot find a willing babysitter for the child, and must take the child to a special occasion such as a church wedding, a small dose of tranquilizer may be prescribed for the child. Some may argue that in these situations, the parents benefit more from the tranquilizer than does the child, as the following anecdote may demonstrate: In the early days of tranquilizers, a distraught mother asked her physician once again for advice regarding her hyperactive 4-year-old son. On previous occasions, she had found her physician's advice neither useful nor practical. On this occasion, the physician told her that there was a new drug in the market which might help. The desperate mother accepted the prescription and left the office. When she returned a month later for a follow up visit, her physician immediately inquired about Johnny, to which she responded with a shrug and a smile: "Who cares?"

In this chapter, we have discussed the medical treatment of ADHD children at some length. It has not been our intention to present stimulant drugs as a panacea. There is no question about the short-term beneficial effects of stimulant drugs. If, however, the hyperactive child can also be taught to gain better control over his own behavior through non-medical means, it would be unreasonable to deny him and his family the benefits of such treatment. Indeed, due to the complexity of ADHD and the heterogeneity of ADHD children, it is best to offer the child and his family a variety of treatment approaches. These will be discussed in the following chapters.

7

Behavioral Approaches to Treatment and Management of ADHD Children

M. Haug

Over the years, many forms of psychological treatment have been tried with ADHD children, but only a few have proven to be of significant benefit for the majority of these children. These fall broadly under the categories of "behavior modification" (also known as "behavior therapy") and "cognitive behavioral therapy."

Behavior Modification

For some people behavior modification has distasteful connotations. They equate it with brain-washing, imposing our will on children, bribing, psychological torture, and forcing children to submission. All of these are, of course, repugnant and far from the truth. Behavior modification is based on the principle that our behavior is influenced and can be changed by the type of response it elicits.

The behavior of a newborn infant is governed primarily by his basic internal drives of hunger, discomfort, pain, etc. As the infant grows, his behavior is increasingly influenced by the behavior and responses of his parents and other people, and in adult life societal norms and rules become major factors governing his behavior. Behavior modification draws upon this basic fact and attempts to bring about a change in the child's behavior by modifying the behavioral responses of parents, teachers and others around him. What follows is a very brief description of the aims and the principles of behavior modification.

Aims

Although behavior modification programs are devised by psychologists or psychiatrists, they are normally carried out by parents and teachers. The professionals teach the principles and procedures of behavior modification to parents and teachers of hyperactive children to assist them in their efforts to bring the child's behavior more into line with societal norms and expectations. The goal is to teach the child how to behave properly, to recognize and follow rules, to cooperate with others, to be a better listener, etc. It is anticipated that when the child learns these skills, he will have more positive and rewarding relationships with other people and will function more productively in the home, school, and community.

Principles

Behavior modification is based on the observation that the behavior of a person (or for that matter, an animal) is governed to a large extent by the consequences that follow the performance of that behavior. If an action is followed by a pleasant or rewarding experience, that action is more likely to be repeated by the person in similar circumstances in the future; the behavior is said to have been "reinforced." If on the other hand, the action is followed by an unpleasant or punishing experience, the action is less likely to recur. Through the application of this basic law of psychology, that is, through a modification of our own responses, we are able to influence one another's behavior. In fact, we cannot escape influencing others or avoid being influenced by others. In the past several decades, much study has been devoted to understanding how we influence one another and what the most effective ways of exerting influences are. We have learned that we can consciously and planfully choose means of interacting with others which would have a greater likelihood of obtaining desired behavioral effects.

Behavior modification makes use of this principle and teaches parents and teachers to more systematically acknowledge and reward the good things the child does (for example, cooperates, pays attention, sits still, plays quietly and completes a task) and to avoid reinforcing his undesirable behaviors. Minor undesirable behaviors should best be ignored. It comes as a surprise to many people that nagging, criticizing, and even spanking may actually reinforce the very behavior they are intended to eliminate! This is because they are all forms of *attention*, and children find attention being paid to them – even the negative kinds of attention, rewarding. It is generally more punishing to a child to be *ignored* than to be "punished!"

If an undesirable behavior can be consistently ignored by everyone in the child's environment, it will often eventually be eliminated or at least reduced to occurring infrequently. If ignoring is ineffective or impractical (as in the case of major infractions of rules of good behavior or potentially dangerous behavior) a procedure called "response-cost" is an effective alternative. In this procedure, the child is given "points" for avoiding undesirable behavior and for engaging in desirable behaviors, which he can exchange for various rewards. Alternatively, he may be given a set number of points at the outset. However, he *loses* a portion of these points every time he displays the undesirable behavior, that is, he suffers a response-cost.

It is important to recognize that the child may never have learned how to perform the desired behaviors or how to perform them well. One can shape the performance of a desired behavior over time by rewarding first the child's effort, then the noted improvements, and finally, the correctly performed behavior.

Using Behavior Modification With the ADHD Child

The same principles apply to the management of the ADHD child's behavior as to that of any other child. However, due to the nature of their disorder, a number of modifications to the general rules are advisable.

1. ADHD children are at the mercy of their impulses. They are not always masters of their own fate. They also have a short attention span and fleeting interests. For these reasons, it is necessary to give the child particularly clear and explicit messages about the behaviors of concern, ensuring that his attention has been drawn to the matter and that he understands the nature of his inappropriate behavior and the purpose of treatment.

2. It is necessary to deliver reinforcements and response-costs swiftly and consistently, so that the child is more likely to note the connection between the behavior and its consequences.

3. Since ADHD children tend to become bored very quickly and easily, one cannot use the same reinforcer for a behavior repeatedly without running the risk of it losing its effectiveness. One must use a variety of rein-

forcers to maintain the child's interest and motivation to perform.

4. Finally, it is helpful to remember that with hyperactive children it is usually better to work on changing one undesirable behavior at a time.

In summary, behavior modification is largely a matter of common sense. However, while simple to explain it is often difficult to put into practice, particularly when there is a long history of negative and coercive interaction between parents and the child. Professional help can be invaluable in helping families to break out of such a pattern and to learn new and more positive ways of influencing one another. It is the most important tool we currently have in treating the preschool age hyperactive child for whom stimulant medication is often not prescribed. It is also a significant supplement for an older child, even one who is responding favorably to stimulant medication, as it maximizes the child's opportunities for learning and for social success as well as developing positive self-esteem.

It is important for parents and teachers to know that the responsibility for changing a child's behavior is theirs; psychologists and psychiatrists can only advise. In particular, the parents must know that their involvement in the treatment program is normally in terms of years rather than weeks or months.

For readers interested in learning more about behavior management, Wesley Becker's book *Parents Are Teachers* is highly recommended.

Limitations of Behavior Therapy

While behavior modification methods are very helpful in improving a child's behavior, they do not in most cases constitute a complete "cure." Their major limitation lies in the fact that the child's behavior remains to a large extent under *external* control – that of parents, teachers, etc., rather than the child himself. The obvious drawback to this is that the child will not always be in the presence of these helpers and particularly as he gets older, he will be called upon more and more to exert self-control.

Other limitations to behavior therapy include the following:

1. The undesirable behavior may recur following cessation of behavior therapy. If the old, pre-treatment reinforcement patterns are resumed, the child's behavior will likely revert back into the old undesirable patterns as well.

2. For a variety of reasons, some hyperactive children do not respond to behavior therapy. Among the more important factors are:

    a) Unless the methods are used very consistently by all persons who interact regularly with the child, their effectiveness is limited.

    b) A child who is a positive responder to medication may become unresponsive to behavior therapy when his medication is discontinued.

    c) If there are serious emotional or interpersonal relationship problems in the family, behavior therapy is unlikely to be successful until these have been addressed.

3. Experience has shown that behavior therapy often is ineffective for children of single parents. Because there are so many competing demands on their time, energy and attention, it is difficult for single parents to apply the procedures with the consistency required in order for them to be effective.

4. It is important for teachers to cooperate with behavior therapy. However, many teachers are unable to carry out a program of behavior modification due to the demands and responsibilities of teaching a large classroom. As is the case with parents, without teachers' commitment to the behavior modification program, it will not work.

5. Finally it must be said that evidence for long term effectiveness of behavior modification is still lacking.

How is Self-Control Acquired?

In the course of normal development, children acquire increasingly sophisticated language skills. They also learn what is known as "inner speech," that is, the ability to form in one's mind a linguistic representation of objects, events, experiences, and relationships. In fact, we all engage in an internal dialogue within ourselves when we think and plan our actions. This internal conversation that we carry on in our minds plays an essential role in shaping our behavior. We can remind ourselves verbally of the consequences of our actions; we can in a sense bring the future symbolically into the present and let it influence our behavior in the here-and-now. Likewise, we can remind ourselves of our past actions and their consequences and use this information to predict the results of various behavioral options and to choose our behavior accordingly. We can also benefit from the accumulated experiences of other people distilled into the form of social norms and rules.

However, ADHD children seem to have difficulty in developing effective control over their behavior through the use of their inner speech. They are often unable to inhibit their responding to the more immediately available gratifications in favor of more distant, but ultimately more satisfying ones. They may "know" the rules; they may have the best of intentions, but they lack the self-control necessary to persist in the pursuit of a long range goal in the face of difficulties or distractions. The poor use of this inner speech also results in their having poor problem–solving skills. Instead of becoming more reflective and planful when "the going gets tough," they tend to become even more hasty, impulsive, and random in their efforts. They do not "talk themselves through" a problem.

Cognitive Behavior Therapy
Aims

Cognitive behavior therapy as applied to impulsive children, including those with ADHD, aims to improve their problem-solving skills and self control through teaching them to use "inner speech" to guide their behavior. They are taught to *monitor* and *evaluate* their own performances, to *instruct* themselves to follow a sequence of steps in problem solving and to provide themselves with appropriate, constructive *consequences* for their own behavior. It is most effective when used with older children, i.e. eight years of age and older, as they are more likely to have the necessary mental maturity to grasp it.

Procedures

Through a combination of discussion, demonstration (modeling by the therapist), and rehearsal, the child is taught a set of verbal self-instructions along the lines of the following:

Step 1 – problem definition:
"Stop! What is the problem?" "What am I supposed to do?"

Step 2 – problem approach:
"I need to make a plan." "What are some plans?" "I have to look at all possibilities." "What are my choices?"

Step 3 – focusing of attention:
"I need to concentrate." This step may be placed either earlier or later in the sequence, depending on the needs of the child.

Step 4 – choosing a response:
"What is the best plan?" "I think this is the answer."

Step 5 – carrying out the response:
"Carry out the plan."

Step 6 – self-evaluation:
"Did the plan work?" "Did I do it right?"

Step 7 – self-reinforcement or coping statement:
"Great! I did a good job!" or "Oh, I made a mistake. Next time I'll go slower and concentrate harder and maybe I will get it right."

The wording, sequence, and number of steps is tailored to the needs and abilities of the individual child, and altered as necessary to fit specific problems. The child practices using the steps, first on impersonal and non-threatening problems such as games, maze puzzles, and school-like tasks (for example, simple arithmetic problems) and then on more emotionally loaded interpersonal problems. Hypothetical problems are role played by the therapist and child or a group of children, using the verbal self instructions to generate more socially appropriate responses. Practice within the therapy sessions is supplemented by "homework" assignments requiring the child to apply these steps to problems encountered at home and at school. Parents and teachers are also taught how to prompt the child to use the steps if he forgets to use them in a situation where they might be helpful.

Like behavior modification, cognitive behavior therapy seems to be an effective tool for improving the behavior of children with ADHD. However, its long term effectiveness has not been established as yet.

Social Skills Training

The above mentioned general self-control training often must be supplemented with specific training in observational skills (recognition of other's feelings, non-verbal social cues, etc.), perspective taking (putting one's self in another's shoes), conversation, and play skills, relaxation, or other areas. The social skill deficits that so often accompany ADHD are often the most troublesome aspects of this disorder. Because of their attention deficit, these children may fail to acquire an awareness and understanding of the subtleties of social interactions; and because of their poor impulse control, they may say and do things that alienate others, often regretting it afterwards, but not profiting from the experience. They may have difficulty in making or in keeping friends, or both. Chronic social failure is likely to lead to demoralization and lowered self-esteem, and the further problems that these create. Thus, it is of vital importance that these children be given direct instructions in the social skills they lack, as it cannot be assumed that they will just "pick them up" the way most children do. Parents and other caring adults should take pains to provide opportunities for social success (for example, through physical education), should assist the child in learning to solve problems as discussed above, and should seek the help of mental health professionals to supplement their efforts where necessary.

8

Parental and Family Issues

C. McFee

In previous chapters we discussed the behavior patterns of children with ADHD and the various approaches to their treatment. In this chapter we will address some of the common concerns of the families of hyperactive children, the effects of the hyperactive child on the family, the family's interaction with the community, and the parents' reaction to the diagnosis. We will also offer some management strategies for the families.

Parents' Common Concerns and Problems

Raising a child with ADHD is a formidible challenge. Most parents of hyperactive children suspect from an early age that their child is different from others and more difficult to handle. However, in their dealing with professionals, they often feel that their concerns are down-played. The parents of hyperactive children, like all other parents, have hopes and dreams of what their children will be and how they, as parents, will play their roles. Many of them experience a sense of failure when their hyperactive child renders the fulfillment of their hopes and dreams difficult. They feel depressed about their inability to control the child's behavior and resent his monopolizing their time and energy. The child becomes identified as the difficult one in the family and the parents come to expect him to misbehave and oppose them.

Self Esteem Issues

Parents who have been successful in raising other children become frustrated when they realize that their parenting skills are ineffective with the ADHD child and the usual praise, rewards, and punishments do not work. They feel a great deal more anxiety and stress when disciplining their hyperactive child than they do when disciplining their other children. They find it difficult to set limits for the ADHD child and maintain order in the home while protecting the rights of other family members. The inability to cope with the demands of the hyperactive child and the pressures that he exerts on the entire family contribute to feelings of inadequacy and diminished self-esteem in many parents.

The child's lowered self-esteem is also a major concern for the parents. The ADHD child often does not see the connection between his behavior and the reactions of others. His annoying behavior frequently leads to rejection by siblings and peers who do not hesitate to "pick on" him whenever the opportunity arises. Faced with a constant stream of negative and defiant behavior, parents find it increasingly difficult to respond positively to the ADHD child. The sense of social failure which arises out of the negative interaction cycle between the child, his parents, siblings, and peers leads to diminished self-esteem. If he happens to experience academic failure as well, his self-esteem will all but disappear.

The Effects of the ADHD Child on the Family

The extraordinary expenditure of time and energy required for parenting an ADHD child, often with few or no measurable results, imposes stress in marital relationships and undermines the family harmony. The conflict and confusion between parents on discipline and how they should respond to the child's demands and annoying behavior can adversely affect the very best parenting intentions. While the parents struggle with their emotional stress in deciding how to respond to the situation, they often respond differently from one another to the same situation. The impact of this conflict on the marital relationship can be significant.

In addition to working through and resolving these differences, parents also need to respond to the siblings' reactions and their stresses. Siblings of an ADHD child often feel neglected due to the attention focused on the ADHD child and are resentful of the different behavioral expectation within the family. They often feel that the ADHD child is the instigator of the conflict or blame him unfairly. The parents, caught in this dilemma, find it difficult to respond rationally in resolving sibling conflicts. Over time, the growing sense of helplessness and frustration can evolve into resentment towards the ADHD child and may increase the risk of parents losing control and physically or emotionally harming the child. When families are troubled by other personal and marital problems, the added stress caused by the behavior of an ADHD child may render them dysfunctional and may lead to eventual family breakdown.

The Effect of External Forces on the Family

Parents of ADHD children often have negative interactions with others outside their immediate family. Extended families (grandparents, uncles, aunts, etc.), friends, neighbors, teachers, and other professionals often confront them about their children's problems and give them unsolicited, conflicting, and confusing advise on how they should raise their children. They come away from these confrontations feeling angry and defensive, believing that they are being held responsible for the child's misbehavior. They perceive hidden messages implying marital problems or poor parenting skills. They hear that they have inappropriate expectations of their children or are not consistent in dealing with bad behavior. They hear veiled accusations of not following through with recommendations for treatment, and lack of love and affection for their children. These negative interactions contribute to the parents' feeling of inadequacy and failure. This often leads to their defensive and sometimes even hostile attitude towards professionals whom they perceive as recommending treatment strategies focused entirely on their deficiencies.

Parents' Reactions to the Diagnosis

Not infrequently the parents of a hyperactive child have consulted a number of physicians or other professionals regarding the child's difficult behavior before ADHD is finally diagnosed. Often there is a two- or three-year lapse from the time the parents suspect that there is something not quite right with their child until the diagnosis is made. During this time, they receive all sorts of well-intentioned, but conflicting and inconsistent advice, often implying poor parenting skills even though they may have raised other healthy and well behaved children. Feelings of frustration, anger, and hostility towards professionals are common in these circumstances.

Parents' reactions vary when at last the diagnosis is explained to them. Some parents feel relieved that they are no longer seen as the cause of their child's problems. Others remain suspicious, confused, and overwhelmed by the amount of information presented to them. Almost all parents struggle with mixed emotions at this time. Even when the diagnosis is thoroughly explained to them, they will wonder whether their child really has little control over his behavior or if he is just uncooperative and stubborn. They still question whether he can hear them well or if, as the doctor explained, his listening skills are what is impaired. They are concerned about his education and future as an adult. They worry that he may become delinquent and eventually end up in prison. They struggle with the difficult decision whether or not they should put him on medication. Dozens of similar questions and concerns regarding the cause, diagnosis, treatment, and prognosis are in their minds. Many parents go home and talk with relatives, friends, and neighbors. They become even more confused when they hear skepticism about the diagnosis, and horror stories about the drugs.

Parents need an opportunity to deal with their mixed emotions. They need time to ask all their questions and absorb all the information. Experienced professionals understand these concerns and emotions and respond appropriately. They know that informed parents are more likely to participate in and comply with the recommended treatment.

Coping With the Problem

The feelings and concerns described above are common and quite normal. They reflect the significant challenge of living with an ADHD child. Understanding these feelings and concerns by both professionals and parents themselves is an essential element of the treatment process. There are no quick and sure cures for attention deficit disorder. However, improvement in the child's behavior and its impact on the health of the family is both possible and realistic. It requires the parents' thorough understanding of ADHD and its implication for the child and the family. It also requires the parents' discovery of their own strengths, to enable them to overcome their frustrations and helplessness.

Identifying Parental Strengths

The first step in coping with the behavior of an ADHD child and the related family problems is for the parents to identify and deal with their own feelings toward the child and to become aware of their own strengths and resources. Many parents of hyperactive children are capable of doing this type of self-analysis with little assistance. However, many other parents have exhausted their inner resources and need to reach out for help to discover their own untapped strengths, to facilitate their problem-solving capacity, and to learn to negotiate new relationships with the larger world which views them negatively. Many parents will benefit from sharing their concerns and their successful coping strategies with other parents of ADHD children. We will further discuss these points in the following pages.

Importance of Consistency and Predictability

As discussed earlier, an ADHD child can have a very stressful impact on the family. The success in reducing this family stress is, to a large extent, dependent on how consistent parents are in dealing with their child's behavior and how rules are determined and enforced. Parents who work as a team and agree upon rules and expectations have a greater probability of success in handling behavior management issues. On the other hand, parents who disagree on rules and expectations undermine their spouse's efforts, create confusion and unpredictability for the child, and reduce their parental authority. In this atmosphere, the child learns to play one parent against the other, increasing dissension and further straining marital relationships. This reinforces the negative interaction cycles within the family and further diminishes the family harmony. Successful parents agree upon realistic rules and attainable goals and work toward gradual and steady improvement rather than striving for instant perfection.

Parental Burn-Out

Parents of hyperactive children commonly state: "We have tried everything, but nothing works for any period of time. We seem to be always angry and find ourselves only responding to his bad behavior." Parents of ADHD children often focus their attention on the child's poor behavior and ignore his appropriate behavior. They exhaust all their other behavior management strategies and rely only on one method, punishment. Eventually, they reach a point where they are physically and emotionally exhausted and sense defeat and helplessness. They are now experiencing "parental burn-out" and are at risk of physically and emotionally harming their child. At this point, they need professional help to cope with their problems.

Seeking Help and Meeting Professionals

Mobilizing resources for the child and the family sometimes becomes a major responsibility for the parents. Communicating the family's needs and advocating their child's needs are often emotionally taxing experiences; especially if parents feel that they are being patronized and not given credit for their assessment. Often parents feel that their physician does not appreciate the depth of the family's concern and does not recognize his own inadequacy to deal with the family's problems. When parents feel a need for referral to another professional or a specialized agency, they often meet resistance. To access resources and services in the community can become a major challenge for the family. The parents' goal in dealing with professionals should be the promotion of a working alliance with them. Of course, this is also the goal of professionals in helping families. To achieve this goal, the parents may find it helpful to utilize the following general strategies:

1. Be prepared for meeting a professional by having a specific goal. Focus on discussing your concerns and do not talk about irrelevant and unrelated topics.

2. Allow the professional to address your concerns one at a time and answer the professional's questions directly,

without wandering off on a tangent. Adopt a listening attitude. Remember their experience with similar situations has given them a different perspective than yours.

3. Refrain from criticizing other professionals regarding their handling of your child's problems as this conveys blaming messages and affects their interest in working with you.

4. Try not to label your child. Instead describe your perception of your child's problems. Leave the diagnosis to the professional, who can come to a proper conclusion if the problem is well described. If the situation improves, let the professional know; positive feedback is important. If the problem continues unabated, ask for another appointment to explore other possibilities. Treatment programs often need to be continuously monitored and modified. Make sure at the outset you learn how often the program is to be reviewed.

Resources for Parents and Families

Many families of ADHD children do well with the assistance of their family physician only. Others will benefit from utilizing other resources in the community. What follows is a brief description of some resources for parents and families of ADHD children. Unfortunately, not all these resources are available in every community.

Parent Counselling. Professional parent counselling services are available in many communities. Parents can access these services through their family physicians, school counsellors, or community health agencies. Parent counselling involves exploring with parents their concerns regarding troublesome behaviors of the ADHD child; providing suggestions for his management, and ways of promoting the development of healthy self-esteem; and generally helping parents with communication and advocacy issues.

Parent Education Workshops. Periodic workshops for parents and others are organized in many communities to provide information on ADHD and to enhance parents', teachers' and others' understanding of this condition as well as the various forms of treatment available for it. If such workshops are not available in the community, parents can get assistance in organizing one by contacting the professional staff of the nearest centre which offers diagnostic and treatment services for ADHD children and their families.

Family Therapy. The goal of family therapy is to explore with the family their conflicts and misunderstandings and to assist the family in coping with their difficulties. Family therapy for ADHD children enhances other forms of treatment. It involves the therapist meeting with the ADHD child and his family to explore how the child's behavior affects each member of the family and helping the family members to utilize their strengths to cope with their emotions.

Family therapy usually requires several sessions. In the initial sessions, the parents and siblings are encouraged to ventilate their feelings and express their frustrations and anger. They are also encouraged to talk about the methods that they have tried to resolve their conflicts. Usually there are many issues, and the therapist helps the family to prioritize these issues and to set realistic goals for themselves. Family members are encouraged to identify their strengths and the therapist, capitalizing on these strengths, suggests alternative means of resolving conflicts. When parents notice recognizable, though small, changes in the family relationships, they further support one another as a team. This strengthens the marital relationship, restores the parents' sense of competence in problem solving, and enhances their self esteem.

ADHD Parent Groups

Some communities have parent support groups for the parents of ADHD children. The objective of these groups is the same as that of parent counselling or family therapy. The groups provide parents with support from other parents and professional group leaders and give them an opportunity to discuss their feelings and problems with other parents experiencing similar difficulties. Often parents trade means of coping with the difficult behavior problems of ADHD children.

At our centre, the parent groups take a problem solving and decision making approach throughout their meetings and concentrate on (1) identification and clarification of issues, (2) development of alternative methods of dealing with issues, (3) implementation of a plan of action, and (4) evaluation of the outcome of these plans.

The parents meet in eight weekly evening sessions with one or two group leaders and often continue meeting on an informal basis following the eight structured meetings.

In the first evening session, the parents are encouraged to share their problems. As opposed to other parent groups, we have found that these ADHD parents groups develop more cohesiveness at a quicker rate due to the intensity of their problems. After telling their "horror stories," they are asked to list at least 15 positive aspects of parenting their children. Initially it is difficult for them to shift away from their negative thinking. Once started, however, they enthusiastically add more descriptors for themselves. These include "challenging, creative, energetic, enthusiastic, empathetic, stronger, patient, involved, accessible, appreciative, assertive, determined, more aware of deficits, need to look for more positives, need to develop more parenting skills."

In the second session, parents are provided with information on the nature of ADHD and its management. Stimulant therapy, behavior therapy, diet or any other form of management that they wish to discuss are discussed. This information helps the parents to clarify any misconceptions that they may have had and to improve their ability to interpret what they read in lay publications or hear from their neighbors and friends. Most of all, it helps them to develop an attitude of coping with the child's problem rather than seeking its cure.

The third session focuses on expectations in extended family, sibling relationships and interactions with others outside the family. In this session we use humor to reduce the stress and enable the parents to see stressful events in a comical light. We make extensive use of cartoons and vignettes by the entertainer Bill Cosby. Humor is an integral part of the therapeutic process. As Mr. Cosby is reported to have said: "Most people don't realize it, but the key to survival as parents is retrospect; retrospect because they were once children and there lies 70% of the answers."

Sessions four, five and six focus on topics pertaining to communication, self esteem, and behavior management. Parents facilitate the process by mutually developing effective problem- solving strategies and drawing upon past successful experiences.

The seventh session deals with parents interaction with schools and the community. Parents-school interactions may evolve into conflict and mutual blaming. The complexity of the child's problem may not be well-understood by school personnel and the child may acquire new maladaptive behaviors in school. This situation can leave both school and parents extremely frustrated. The emphasis for this session is to promote a positive approach to communication with schools with a view to cooperative problem solving. An education consultant is brought in at this session to review with the parents the available local resources and the appropriate lines of communication with schools and school boards.

In the final session, the parents are encouraged to give feedback, share their feelings about the group process, and identify areas which they felt were beneficial and those which were not. Group leaders also give feedback supporting individual group members and maximizing their potential in terms of problem- solving, self awareness and decision making. Verbal feedback and completion of questionnaires by parents are used to evaluate the content and the process of group sessions. This information is then used for planning future groups.

Our experience with parent support groups has convinced us that it is a very effective supplemental mode of treatment which helps parents to understand ADHD and cope with their day-to-day stress and difficulties. Initially parents are concerned with the child and his behavior; as the sessions progress, parents focus more on themselves, seeking out their own hidden strengths to help the child. Parents report that as a result of their group experience they feel more in control when handling the ADHD child and better able to communicate within the family. They also become more accepting of one another and more confident in their parenting roles.

Although we have not had a sufficiently long experience to know the effects of the family support groups on children's prognosis, published research evidence from other investigators indicates that understanding, accepting and supportive families have a positive and favorable influence on the long term prognosis of children with ADHD.

9

Teaching ADHD Children

S. Gupta

Teaching a child with ADHD is a major challenge for most teachers. In addition to the normal demands of the classroom, the teacher is required to deal with the disruptive and non-compliant behavior of the hyperactive child and to help him with his academic progress, a most difficult task, indeed.

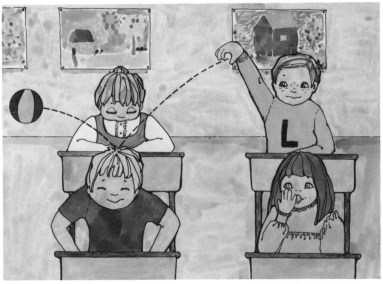

The principles of behavior management are outlined in Chapter 7 and are applicable both at home and at school.

Normal children learn with relative ease the rules of appropriate behavior and the learning tasks in school. ADHD children, on the other hand, have to be repeatedly taught how to listen, when and how to be on task, how to solve problems, how to complete assignments, why and how not to interrupt, and how to control their emotions. The majority of teachers are familiar with techniques of accomplishing these formidable tasks and use them effectively. Some teachers take advantage of the challenge of teaching an ADHD child to improve their own teaching and interpersonal skills. A few find the presence of an ADHD child in the classroom too disruptive and experience difficulty fulfilling the challenge and the call of their profession. What follows is a brief outline of strategies which teachers may find useful in dealing with a few common scenarios that teachers face when they have an ADHD child in their class.

A. The child daydreams, does not seem to listen, and does not follow directions.

Most of us take the ability to listen for granted since normal children have no difficulty listening. Listening implies focusing attention on what is being said and ignoring all other irrelevant sounds and sights; skills that most ADHD children have not acquired. Listening skills can be organized and taught under three headings: prelistening strategies, strategies that can be used during the listening process, and those which can be used after listening.

Prelistening strategies can be taught by establishing a definite purpose for the lesson. This can be done verbally and by outlining it on the board. The aim here is to develop a motivation for learning. The teacher must assure that the ADHD child's attention is drawn and focused on the purpose of the lesson. Periodic verbal reminders or still better, agreed upon non-verbal cues may be necessary for the ADHD child to listen or to remain on–task. For example, if the child is not listening and is preoccupied with another activity, the teacher can walk over and gently touch his shoulder. Each teacher, however, must decide on strategies that she is comfortable with and thinks will work. This may be a gesture, a word or a look.

To facilitate the development of listening skills, it is important for the teacher to organize the information being presented. This can be done by highlighting what is going to be discussed. When the information presented is organized according to time or sequence, it is less confusing for the ADHD child and this facilitates his listening. The ADHD children, more than normal children, need to know not only what it is that they are required to learn, but also its relevance by explicitly relating vocabulary and concepts to the child's background experience. Half of the battle is won if the teacher can engage the child.

Postlistening skills can be taught by using verbal rehearsal with direct instruction: "Repeat in your own words . . ." and by using visual imagery: "Make a picture in your own head." They can be encouraged to infer meaning by anticipating why, how, what, and where questions.

Since ADHD children find it very difficult to pay attention, it is important for a teacher to pace instruction so that it is not too fast or too slow and that it follows a sequential order. ADHD children cannot remember more than one or two instructions at a time and learn better in direct instruction rather than in discovery learning.

B. The child cannot start a task and complete it

To encourage on–task behavior and completion of task, the teacher can give reinforcement on a fixed schedule, that is, at regular intervals or after a set number of responses. Reinforcers are briefly discussed in Chapter 7 and include anything which tends to increase the frequency of a desired behavior. For example, verbal praise such as "Good John, you worked two minutes quietly," encourages on-task behavior. If a child is doing a mathematic problem, he is asked to complete one or two problems only and not the entire sheet. When the child completes this, he is praised and asked to complete the next two problems. The teacher can gradually increase expectation until the child learns to complete the entire task. In doing so, the teacher allows the child every opportunity to be successful.

C.   The child is disruptive in the class

To deal with the disruptive behavior of an ADHD child, the teacher must ignore as much of this behavior as possible. Paying attention to inappropriate behavior may be a reinforcer for an ADHD child. Ignoring it, on the other hand, will more quickly lead to the "extinction" of that behavior. Non-verbal cues that the teacher and student have agreed upon can be used as a signal to help the child to realize that what he is doing is not acceptable. The teacher may anticipate the child's behavior and go over to the child to quietly remind him. Often the teacher's presence stops the disruptive behavior. When the child makes noises, giggles, coughs, etc., the teacher can ask the child to run an errand to perform some other chores in the classroom. This is a useful technique which allows the child to discontinue the disruptive behavior. At the same time, the teacher does not appear punitive, causing embarrassment to the child and eliciting his anger.

D.   The child has frequent temper tantrums

Tantrums have several stages and each stage must be dealt with differently. The first stage is the grumbling stage. The teacher usually recognizes a pattern of events which may lead to the child's tantrum. For example, the teacher recognizes that the child becomes angry before or after a certain activity. She can help the child to verbalize his problems and this often prevents a full blown tantrum. Without drawing attention to the child, the teacher can walk over to him and say "I think you are upset and I am wondering if ... happened as you were walking in just now. Let's see how you can make it different for yourself so you are not upset."

The second stage is the noisy stage when the child is aware of breaking the rules and is signalling for help. The child seems to be seeking external control. At this time, it is necessary for the teacher not to say that the child is breaking the rules, but help him to signal his needs for help in a more appropriate manner. The teacher may say "I know you are angry. You can have quiet time for two minutes at your desk."

During the next stage, the full blown temper, the child usually refuses to accept any suggestions the teacher may make. It may not be possible to manage his tantrum and may be necessary to remove him from the classroom.

The next stage is the "leave me alone stage" and it is best to leave the child alone during this stage to allow him to regain his control.

In the last stage, the child has regained control over his emotions. During this stage, the teacher can help the child to develop alternate coping skills. He can be helped to find answers to the following questions:

1. What did you do that got you into trouble?
2. What did you expect to gain by doing what you did?
3. How could you have got what you wanted without getting into trouble?

The use of these techniques is demanding and requires a great deal of patience and planning.

The Use of Cognitive Behavior Therapy in Teaching ADHD Children

As stated in Chapter 7, behavior modification techniques require a change of response to the inappropriate behavior and/or a restructuring of the environment. This may be a disadvantage in that the child may learn to become dependent on external controls to behave according to the rules of the classroom or societal norms. Cognitive behavior therapy on the other hand, teaches the child self control. The techniques of cognitive behavior therapy can also be used for classroom instruction. The child is taught to "think out loud" and use self-guiding verbalizations, self–monitoring, and self-reinforcement in solving problems. Various steps of cognitive behavioral therapy are outlined in Chapter 7 and will not be repeated here. The following examples should serve to demonstrate how this approach can be used for instructions.

"A boy bought five pieces of gum at 9¢ each. How much did he spend?"

The student thinks aloud:

1. What am I supposed to do? I am supposed to know how much money the boy spent.

2. What are the possibilities? He spent more than 9¢ because he bought five pieces. I can either add or multiply.

3. I must concentrate on what is the best way of finding the answers.

4. I must choose the right answer, I think I will multiply,

5. self monitoring – I think I did it right.

6. self reinforcement – I did a good job because I thought it through. Or, I did not get the right answer. I will try harder the next time.

A similar approach can be used in interpersonal situations. For example, Billy is knocked down by Joey in the playground. Billy's first impulse is to punch Joey. Instead, he is taught to ask himself:

1. What is the problem? I am angry because Joey knocked me down.

2. What can I do? I can punch Joey, but that will get me into trouble. I can ignore Joey, but that is difficult and I remain angry. I can talk to the teacher and he can talk to Joey. Or, I can talk to Joey myself and tell him I don't like to be knocked down and will not put up with it in the future.

3. Focusing attention. I must think and choose the best answer to my problem.

4. Choosing the best answer. I think I will talk to Joey myself.

5. Self reinforcement. I am proud of myself for not allowing my anger to get me into trouble.

Problem–solving approaches have been used in many

school curriculum guides for teachers. A particularly useful one is "Elementary Mathematics Curriculum Guide" developed by the Alberta Department of Education. It consists of four basic steps associated with the problem solving process, namely understanding the problem, developing a plan, carrying out the plan and looking back. Within each step are problem solving strategies which assist in the thinking through and solving of problems. These strategies are outlined in the following table. It is not intended that all of these strategies be dealt with in the earlier grades. Interested teachers should consult this curriculum guide for grade–by–grade treatment of the problem–solving component.

Steps in the Problem Solving Process

Understand the Problem	Develop a Plan	Carry out the Plan	Looking Back
Strategies	**Strategies**	**Strategies**	**Strategies**
1. Use Actions	1. Look for Patterns	1. Identify Objects	1. Check Groups Sorted
2. Interpret a Picture	2. Collect and Organize Data (tally and/or graphs)	2. Use Organized Data	2. Discuss Solutions
3. Identify Key Words	3. Act it Out	3. Continue the Pattern	3. Check the Pattern
4. Use Manipulatives	4. Use Manipulatives	4. Use Manipulatives to Show Solutions	4. Retell the Problem with Solutions
5. Ask Questions	5. Write a Number Sentence	5. Solve Using Mathematical Symbols	5. Account for Other Possibilities
6. Restate in Your Own Words	6. Choose the Appropriate Operation	6. Perform Actions in a Problem	6. Make and Solve Similar Problems
7. Identify Wanted and Given Information	7. Guess and Check	7. Interpret the Plan	7. Explain the Solution
8. Identify Needed Information	8. Identify Relationships	8. Identify Relationships	8. Check the Solution
9. Identify Extraneous Information	9. Sketch and Plan	9. Employ the Four Step Problem Solving Approach	9. Find Another Way to Solve It
10. Change Your Point of View	10. Set up a Mathematical Condition	10 Interpret Formulas	10. Generalize Your Solution
11. Look for Hidden Assumptions	11. Do a Simpler but Related Problem	11. Make a Flow Chart	11. Verify Formulas
	12. Use Logic or Reason	12. Make a Diagram	
	13. Collect Outside Information		
	14. Exhaust all Possibilities		
	15. Devise a Formula		
	16. Review Steps Taken		

Elementary Mathematics Curriculum Guide, 1982. Alberta Education, Edmonton, Alberta.

10

Other Approaches to the Treatment of ADHD.

Diet and Hyperactivity

In the 1970s, the widespread protest against "drugging" school children was still loud and intensive. During the same period, the back-to-nature movement was also gaining momentum. The time was right for the introduction of a different approach to the management of ADHD which, in spite of successes of stimulant therapy, had remained a major challenge for all professionals. Dr. Ben Feingold of San Francisco, impressed by the successful treatment

of aspirin-sensitive adults with a diet which was free of naturally- occurring salicylates (aspirin or ASA is acetylsalicylic acid), hypothesized that hyperactive and learning-disabled children might also respond to this treatment. Clinical experience had shown that tartrazine, a yellow food coloring, could induce identical clinical patterns in aspirin-sensitive individuals, even though the two substances are not chemically or structurally related. In some patients, the exclusion of foods which contained naturally-occurring salicylates did not improve their clinical picture, but did so when tartrazine was also excluded. However, some patients continued with their problems, even when they were on a diet which was free of both naturally-occurring salicylates and tartrazine. Dr. Feingold then hypothesized that, since literally thousands of food colorings, flavorings and preservatives in the market are added to our foods, some of them, though chemically not related to tartrazine or aspirin, might be responsible for the clinical picture of aspirin sensitivity. This was the basis for the introduction of his K-P diet (Kaiser- Permanente Medical Centre where Dr. Feingold worked), which was salicylate and additive free. He claimed that a number of conditions, involving skin, respiratory, gastrointestinal, neurological and skeletal systems, were manifestations of adverse reactions to some naturally occurring substances in food and/or food additives. He further hypothesized that adverse reactions occur only in certain genetically- predisposed, sensitive individuals.

Dr. Feingold initially claimed that a large number of hyperactive and learning disabled children responded to the K-P diet, and that they showed a marked deterioration in their behavior following the re-introduction of the offensive foods. In 1975 he published his well-known and popular book: "Why Your Child is Hyperactive." The time for this book was right, and many parents and professionals, including many physicians who objected to stimulant therapy, resorted to the use of the K-P diet. Since that time, all professionals working with hyperactive children have heard many stories of disappointment as well as dramatic improvement in the behavior of some hyperactive children following dietary modifications.

IN GOD WE TRUST
EVERYONE ELSE MUST HAVE DATA

The history of medicine is replete with claims of success in the treatment of all sorts of ailments. Medical scientists, however, have long learned not to accept anecdotal or testimonial evidence until their validity is scientifically demonstrated. There is nothing wrong with anecdotes or testimonials. They are the initial observations which form the impetus for all scientific inquiries. Scientists draw inferences based on their observations and develop hypotheses. When a hypothesis is developed, they set up experiments to either prove or disprove it. In medicine, claims of treatment success are subjected to rigorous tests before they are either accepted as useful or rejected. Throughout the history of science, and particularly during the twentieth century, scientists have become increasingly sophisticated in their design of experiments. The experimental studies of the effectiveness of various forms of treatment of hyperactivity are examples of this sophistication.

Since we can all be biased either in favor of or against any form of treatment and our bias can influence our observations, experimental studies must be designed in such a way as to eliminate this bias. Double-blind methods, in which neither the investigators nor the persons who are being treated know who is receiving a treatment claimed to be effective and who is receiving an ineffective placebo, are the cornerstone of these experimental designs.

When the effectiveness of a drug is being investigated, it is relatively easy to produce a placebo with the same size, shape, color and taste to counteract this bias factor. Investigation of the effectiveness of dietary modifications is not that easy. How does one prevent the child from raiding the refrigerator or the cookie jar? How does one ascertain that the child does not eat a candy, or something else, given to him by his friends? How does one hide the color or taste of foods, if food colorings, flavor enhancers, or food preservatives are removed from or added to the child's food? These are a few of many difficulties which have been associated with studies of diet and its relationship to behavior. Many techniques have been used to overcome these difficulties. These include the removal of all foods from the home, and supplying the family's entire food requirement for several weeks. During this time, the food is manipulated without the family's knowledge.

Almost all of these studies have been criticized for "methodological flaws," that is, imperfections in the study designs which make it difficult to draw valid conclusions from them. In addition, in the scientific circles, the results of even the most well- designed studies are often not readily accepted, until similar results are obtained in replicated studies by other researchers elsewhere. A few well-designed studies, however, have demonstrated that some hyperactive children show an improvement in their behavior following dietary modifications, and that this improvement does not seem to be a placebo effect. Our own studies of hyperactive preschool children have demonstrated similar results. Unfortunately, no one can predict which child may benefit from dietary modifications. Current research in a number of centres indicates that there is a tremendous variability in children's response to dietary substances. A great deal of research is still required to clarify many unanswered questions regarding the effect of diet and dietary modification on hyperactive children's behavior.

Since the introduction of the K-P diet, panels of experts in the United States, consisting of well known researchers from many fields, have reviewed the evidence derived from the studies on the relationship between diet and hyperactivity. Their conclusions have been similar; namely, further research is required to establish this relationship. This, of course, does not mean that there is no relationship between food and human behavior. It merely means that the relationship between the behavior of hyperactive children and food additives or naturally-occurring substances in food has not been conclusively demonstrated.

Notwithstanding the above critique of dietary modification for the treatment of hyperactive children, many parents remain convinced that their children have benefited from the K-P diet and many more parents request similar dietary modification for their children. Since additive-free diets have not been associated with any harmful effects, there is no reason to discourage families who wish to pursue such a diet. Diets which are free of naturally-occurring salicylates, however, are very restrictive and can result in nutritional deficiencies, if they are not under the supervision of a trained dietitian. Parents must ensure that their children are receiving the recommended minimum daily amounts of essential nutrients. It is imperative that parents consult their family physicians or pediatricians before embarking on this type of diet. Many physicians, however, remain opposed to dietary modification for the treatment of hyperactivity and will advise against it. If, in spite of the advice of their physicians, parents wish to pursue this diet, they can obtain assistance regarding their child's nutritional requirements from their local health departments. The local associations for children and adults with learning disabilities may also provide some help.

Dr. Feingold has published a second book, "The Feingold Cookbook for Hyperactive Children" which the parents may find useful. It must be emphasized that it is difficult to give any restrictive diet of this nature to only one member of the family. Usually the diet of the entire family must be changed and this may place the family under a great deal of stress.

The relationship between behavior and certain neurotransmitters in the brain was mentioned previously in this book. There are a few studies which show that increasing certain normal dietary components which are the precursors (building blocks) of these neurotransmitters increases their concentration in the brain. Therapeutic effectiveness of this type of dietary modification, however, has not been demonstrated and requires further research.

Sugar as a Cause of Hyperactivity

Many parents also claim dramatic improvements in their children's behavior when they are put on a restricted sugar intake. Again, this is testimonial evidence and as such provides impetus for scientific research. Blind studies carried out on the effect of sugar on children's behavior have demonstrated only the placebo effect of this treatment. In other words, when mothers are blind to the experiment, that is, they do not know whether the child is receiving sugar or an artificial sweetener in his food or drink, their rating of the child's behavior does not correspond with what the child is actually taking.

Once again, since sugar is not an essential component of the human diet, one cannot discourage parents who wish to pursue a low sugar diet for their children from doing so. More rational advice regarding sugar, food additives and a salicylate-free diet can be given only when future research clarifies many as yet unanswered questions.

Megavitamin Therapy

There are some individuals with genetic deficits who, in order to function normally, require greater amounts of certain nutrients than is required by the general population. A number of disorders are known to fall into this category. Based on this knowledge, some observers have suggested that some brain dysfunctions might also be caused by this type of "deficiency." Megavitamin therapy for the treatment of schizophrenia is an example of this belief and still has its supporters, in spite of the fact that scientific research has not proven its efficacy. Hyperactivity has also been postulated by some to be caused by a genetically-determined increased need for some vitamins. Once again, well-designed scientific research has not proven the efficacy of megavitamin therapy in the management of ADHD. In fact, a recent study demonstrated adverse effects of large doses of some water-soluable vitamins which until now have been considered relatively harmless. For this reason, megavitamin therapy should be avoided until further research has clearly demonstrated its efficacy and safety, when used over prolonged periods of time.

It must be emphasized that when the child is given any form of treatment, whether stimulant therapy, K-P diet, low sugar diet, or megavitamin therapy, the benefits and potential harms for the child and his family must be carefully considered. Some forms of treatment may deprive the child of a more effective and proven means of treatment. Other forms of treatment may create a great deal of family stress. This may be the case when, for the sake of treating the child, his entire family is placed on a diet which may be stressful, distasteful and offensive to other family members.

11

Prognosis:
When ADHD Children Grow Up

The wildest colts make the best horses.

Themistocles
512 – 449 B.C.

There are many published studies on the outcome of childhood hyperactivity in adolescence and adulthood. Most of these studies suffer from limitations which are associated with all long-term follow-up studies and which make it difficult to draw valid conclusions from them. These limitations include the following:

1.   ADHD children are a mixed bag of individuals. In some, hyperactivity is a prominent feature; in others, it is less prominent or absent. Some ADHD children are highly intelligent; others are less intelligent. Some have a passive disposition; others are aggressive. Some have understanding and patient parents, others do not. Some have been treated adequately, others less so. They all have had different upbringings. If all ADHD children are lumped together for outcome studies, it would be difficult to interpret the results of such studies, since each subgroup of these children may have a different prognosis.

2.   One of the most troublesome aspects of outcome studies is the lack of information about that segment of the ADHD population which is lost to follow up. Follow-up studies are

usually done on children attending hospital-based clinics. Many ADHD children and their families do not keep their return clinic appointments a few months or so after their initial assessment. If only those ADHD children who are responsive to treatment and faithfully return to clinics are included in outcome studies, one cannot be sure whether the conclusions drawn from these studies can be applied to all ADHD children. Those who are lost to follow up are not necessarily similar to those who are followed; they may be different with respect to their initial symptoms, their intelligence, the strength of their families, and many other factors which might influence their prognosis.

3. Another troublesome problem in outcome studies is that we do not know how well ADHD children and their families comply with the recommended treatment. In one study of compliance with the drug therapy, the children's urine was tested for the presence of the prescribed drugs. A large percentage of urine samples showed no trace of the prescribed medications. If we do not know how well the ADHD children and their families follow through with recommended treatment, it is meaningless to draw conclusions from outcome studies about the differences between those who ostensibly were treated and those who were not.

4. The length of treatment of ADHD children obviously affects their prognosis. In outcome studies further difficulties arise from the fact that the majority of ADHD children who take their medications more or less faithfully, do so for only a few years. They discontinue their medication either on the recommendation of their physicians or at their own initiative. This is because many ADHD children are no longer visibly hyperactive in their adolescence and adulthood, even though they may continue having impulsivity and attentional problems. Many outcome studies on the effectiveness of stimulant therapy have found that ADHD children have a poor prognosis in terms of educational achievement and social adjustment. These findings, however, should be interpreted with caution. If stimulant therapy is discontinued only because

hyperactivity is no longer a major problem, the persistence of impulsivity and attentional problems into adulthood cannot be attributed to the ineffectiveness of this form of treatment. One cannot conclude that ADHD has an inherently poor prognosis. It can only be said that short-term stimulant therapy is ineffective in permanently eliminating impulsivity and attentional problems. The point is that some ADHD children require treatment for their inattention and impulsivity in their adolescence and adulthoods, even if they are no longer hyperactive. Without their medications, they continue to experience academic and social difficulties.

Many of the past outcome studies drew a relatively gloomy picture for ADHD children. ADHD children were seen as individuals who would not fare well as adults. Frequently, disappointments were expressed about the lack of long-term benefits of stimulant therapy, in spite of its obvious short-term benefits. These disappointments were based on the false expectation that stimulants would cure the disorder, or with maturation ADHD children would outgrow their problems. Some of these initial studies indicated that aggression in ADHD children was an indicator of a poor prognosis, since about one half of the aggressive ADHD children developed antisocial problems in their adolescence. These studies do not tell us, however, why the other half of aggressive ADHD children did not develop antisocial problems. Nor do they tell us what happened to many aggressive ADHD children who were lost for follow up. Many of these studies also did not follow ADHD children long enough in order to know what happened to them in adulthood.

With these limitations in mind, we can now look at one of the better outcome studies which has been carried out by investigators at the Montreal Children's Hospital. They have published the results of their five, ten, and fifteen-year follow-up studies of hyperactive children seen in their clinic. These studies included information obtained from the affected individuals, their parents, teachers, school counsellors, and employers, as well as psychiatric interviews of the individuals, IQ and other psychometric assessments, height, weight, pulse and blood pressure measurements and electroencephalo-grams. Although over the years, their loss to follow-up was relatively significant (fifteen years following the initial assessment, only 61 out of the original group of 104 individuals were available for follow up) some interesting results were published.

Their five-year follow-up group included 22 children who were treated with *chlorpromazine* (a tranquillizer) for 18 months to five years, 24 children who were treated with *methylphenidate* –Ritalin, for three to five years and 22 children who received no treatment. There was no significant difference between the treated and untreated hyperactive children in measurements of their emotional adjustment, delinquency, intelligence and other psychometric tests. However, those children who were treated with Ritalin were more manageable at home and at school.

The ten-year follow-up included 76 hyperactive children and 45 normal children who served as controls for comparison with hyperactive children. The 75 hyperactive children had received varying lengths and types of drug therapy and some had received individual psychotherapy. However, the investigators reported that, "In general, this group represented a relatively untreated group, with few receiving adequate counselling or drug therapy." In other words the ten-year follow-up compares normal children with a relatively untreated group of hyperactive children. The ten-year follow-up results indicated that the original 75 hyperactive children can be divided into three subgroups of young adults. The first group, consisting of nearly 50% of the original group, had outgrown their symptoms and were functioning normally. The second group, also about 50% of the total, continued to have significant problems of impulsivity and hyperactivity which interfered to varying degrees with their work and interpersonal functioning and were associated with low self-esteem. The third group was a small, statistically insignificant, group who showed borderline personality disorders. It must be reiterated that these were young adults who in childhood were diagnosed as hyperactive and, for all intents and purposes, did not receive adequate treatment.

In a separate ten to twelve-year follow-up report, these investigators compared 20 children who had received at least three years of treatment with methylphenidate with normal controls. The results indicated that in many areas such as school, work and personality disorders, stimulant-treated hyperactives functioned significantly worse than controls but similar to untreated hyperactives. In some areas such as less car accidents, more positive view of childhood, less delinquency and better social skills and self-esteem, stimulant-treated hyperactives did better than their untreated counterparts.

The fifteen-year follow-up included 61 of the original 104 hyperactive children and 41 of 45 normal controls. The results indicated that about 50% of the hyperactives continued to have mild to severely disabling symptoms. Twenty-three percent of the 61 individuals reported some traits of antisocial personality disorder (please note that this was based on self-administered questionnaires completed by the previously diagnosed hyperactive individuals; *they did not all have antisocial behavior!*). Schizophrenia, alcoholism, or alcohol and drug abuse were not found more commonly in the hyperactive group, but hyperactives functioned generally less well than normal controls. Those who had antisocial behavior at fifteen-year follow-up had early and persistent histories of antisocial behavior. However, many hyperactives did not continue their antisocial behavior into adulthood. There appears to be a small subgroup of hyperactive individuals who have more negative outcomes.

A very interesting finding of this study is that, although antisocial behavior, if present early in life, continues in many (but not all) of these individuals, by itself it is not a predictor of a poor outcome in adulthood. The outcome is more dependent on the interactions and cumulative effect of a number of factors including aggressivity, IQ, emotional instability, socioeconomic status of the family, and the mental health of the family members. This finding underscores the importance of

100 Attention Deficit Disorder

an understanding and supportive family in influencing the adult outcome of hyperactivity.

It is very important to remember that many of the so-called treated individuals in the Montreal study did not receive adequate treatment. Would there be any difference between the controls and hyperactive individuals, if the latter group had received adequate treatment for as long as their symptoms persisted? This, of course, cannot be answered through the Montreal follow up study.

The Montreal investigators have published the results of their entire study, with a review of the literature on the adult outcome of hyperactivity: "Hyperactive Children Grown Up." This book provides interesting reading for anyone who is interested in the prognosis of attention-deficit hyperactivity disorder.

At the present time, we have no solid evidence about the poor outcome of hyperactivity in adulthood. What we do know is that some of the untreated or inadequately treated hyperactive children do not do as well as non-hyperactive children in adulthood. There is evidence, however, which suggests that even inadequate treatment improves their prognosis. Until we have better information about the prognosis, it is prudent to continue with a treatment which has proven its effectiveness for as long as the symptoms persist. In the meantime, the following story should help those of us who prefer to remain optimistic:

> *According to the theory of aerodynamics, and as may be readily demonstrated through laboratory tests and wind tunnel experiments, the bumblebee is unable to fly. This is because the size, weight and shape of his body in relation to the total wing spread makes flying impossible. But the bumble bee, being ignorant of these profound scientific truths, goes ahead and flies anyway . . . and manages to make a little honey everyday!*

Suggested Readings

For a more detailed discussion of the topics in this book, the readers may refer to the following books.

Barkley, R.A. *Hyperactive Children: A Handbook for Diagnosis and Treament*. Guilford Press, Now York, 1981.

Becker, W.C. *Parents are Teachers*. Research Press, Champaign, Illinois, 1971.

Briggs, D.C. *Your Child's Self–Esteem*. Dolphin Books (Doubleday and Co.), New York, 1975.

Elementary Mathematics Curriculum Guide, 1982. Alberta Education, Edmonton, Alberta.

Fontenelle, D.H. *Understanding and Managing Overactive Children*. Prentice Hall, Englewood Cliffs, NJ, 1983.

Fry, P.S. and Lupart, J.L. *Cognitive Process in Childrn's Learning: Practical Applications in Education Practice and Classroom Management*. Charles C. Thomas, SpringField, Illinios, 1987.

Kirby, E.A. and Grimley, L.K. *Understanding and Treating Attention Deficit Disorder*. Pergamon Press, Toronto, 1986.

Kendall, P.C. and Braswell, L. *Cognitive–Behavioral Therapy for Impulsive Children*. Guilford Press, New York, 1985.

Levine, M.D., Brooks, R. and Shonkoff, J.P. *A Pediatric Approach to Learning Disorders*. John Wiley and Sons, New York, 1980.

Sleator, E.K. and Pelham, W.E. Jr. *Attention Deficit Disorder*. Appleton–Century–Croft. Norwalk, Conneticut, 1986.

Swift, M.S. and Spivack, G. *Alternative Teaching Strategies: Helping Behaviorally Troubled Children Achieve*. Research Press, Champaign, Illinios, 1975.

Weiss, G. and Hechtman, L.T. *Hyperactive Children Grown Up*. Guilford Press, New York, 1986.